READ WELL Plus

Space School

Teacher's Guide

Unit 47

Note: See objectives on page 2 for a complete list of skills taught and reviewed.

Critical Foundations in Primary Reading

Marilyn Sprick and Shelley V. Jones

ISBN 1-59318-470-0

10 09 08 07 06 05 1 2 3 4 5 6

SOPRIS WEST™ EDUCATIONAL SERVICES
A CAMBIUM LEARNING COMPANY

BOSTON, MA • LONGMONT, CO

Table of Contents

Unit 47

Space School

How to Teach the Lessons

How to Teach the Lessons (*continued*)

End of the Unit

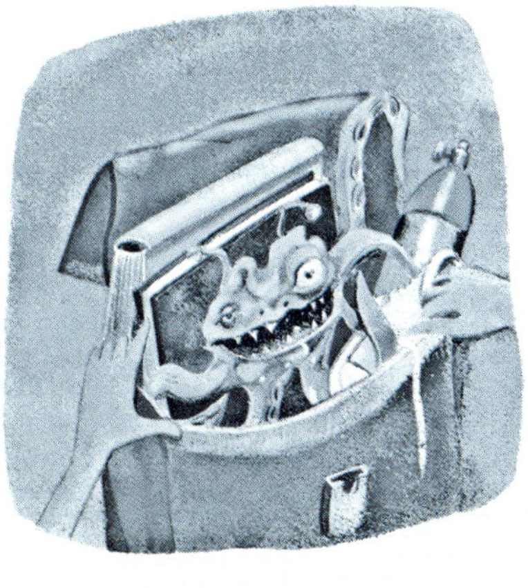

Letter Sounds and Combinations

Cumulative Review of *Read Well 1* Letter Sounds and Combinations

Ss, Ee, ee, Mm, Aa, Dd, th, Nn, Tt, Ww, Ii, Th, Hh, Cc, Rr, ea, sh, Sh, Kk, -ck, oo, ar, wh, Wh, e (short), *-y* (as in "fly"), *Ll, Oo, Bb, all, Gg, Ff, Uu, er, oo* (as in "book"), *Yy, a* (schwa), *Pp, ay, Vv, Qq, Jj, Xx, or, Zz, a_e, -y* (as in "baby"), *i_e, ou, ow, ch, Ch, ai, igh, o_e, ir*

aw /aw/ **Paw** Voiced **Unit 39**	ew /ew/ **Crew** Voiced **Unit 40**	u_e /oo/ **Blue** Bossy E Voiced (Long) **Unit 40**	ōw /ōw/ **Snow** Voiced (Long) **Unit 41**	ge /j/ **Page** Voiced **Unit 42**	ci /sss/ **Circle** Unvoiced **Unit 43**
ce /sss/ **Center** Unvoiced **Unit 43**	Kn/kn /nnn/ **Knee** Voiced **Unit 44**	Ph/ph /fff/ **Phone** Unvoiced **Unit 44**	oa /oa/ **Boat** Voiced (Long) **Unit 45**	oi /oi/ **Point** Voiced **Unit 46**	ĕa /ĕa/ **Bread** Voiced (Short) **Unit 46**
au /au/ **Astronaut** Voiced **Unit 48**	gi /j/ **Giraffe** Voiced **Unit 48**	oy /oy/ **Boy** Voiced **Unit 49**	-dge /j/ **Badge** Voiced **Unit 50**		

Affixes (including Morphographs—affixes taught with meaning) and Open Syllables

Cumulative Review of *Read Well 1* Affixes

-ed, -en, -er, -es, -est, -ing, -ly, -s, -y, -tion

re- **Means "again"** as in "reread" **Unit 39**	un- **Means "not"** as in "unhappy" **Unit 40**	ex- as in "excite" **Unit 40**	-ful **Means "full of"** as in "colorful" **Unit 41**	o- Open Syllable /ō/ as in "open" and "moment" **Unit 41**	bi- **Means "two"** as in "bicycle" **Unit 42**
de- as in "detective" **Unit 43**	-able as in "comfortable" **Unit 44**	i- Open Syllable /ī/ as in "silence" and "pilot" **Unit 47**	be- as in "before" **Unit 48**	dis- as in "discover" **Unit 49**	-ous as in "enormous" **Unit 49**

Introduction
Space School

Story Notes

Everyone has had a problem before. However, most people haven't had the kind of problem Asha (Aw-shuh) has in her backpack. Asha and her friend Maria try to figure out what to do with a problem that could eat Asha's backpack, her air tank, and perhaps even the space shuttle. This futuristic story, set in a world of robots, space travel, and aliens, will tickle students' curiosity about the possibilities of future space travel.

Recommended Read Aloud

For reading outside of small group instruction

The Magic School Bus: Lost in the Solar System
by Joanna Cole

Fiction • Narrative

When the planetarium is closed, Ms. Frizzle's class rockets off into space for an up-close viewing of all of the planets in the Solar System. The students have to take over when Ms. Frizzle is unexpectedly lost in space.

***Read Well* Connection**

"A Problem in a Backpack" and *The Magic School Bus: Lost in the Solar System* tell engaging tales about space that excite students' imaginations. Students learn about real-life technology as well as factual information about the Solar System and space travel.

NOTE FROM THE AUTHORS

GUEST AUTHOR

Author Jerry Oltion has written 15 novels (including four Star Trek novels) and more than 100 short stories. In 1997, Jerry won the Nebula Award for best novella. "A Problem in A Backpack" is Jerry's first story for young children. We hope it won't be his last.

COMMENT FROM JERRY'S YOUNGEST FAN

"I like the space school story. It was my favorite story. Thank you for letting us read this story."

—Corey

New and Important Objectives

A Research-Based Reading Program

Just Right for Young Children

Phonemic Awareness
Phonics
Fluency
Vocabulary
Comprehension

Phonological and Phonemic Awareness

Isolating Beginning, Middle, Ending Sounds, Segmenting, Blending, Rhyming, Onset and Rime, Counting Syllables

Phonics

Cumulative Letter Sounds and Combinations

Review • *Ss, Ee, ee, Mm, Aa, Dd, th, Nn, Tt, Ww, Ii, Th, Hh, Cc, Rr, ea, sh, Sh, Kk, -ck, oo, ar, wh, Wh, e* (short), *-y* (as in "fly"), *Ll, Oo, Bb, all, Gg, Ff, Uu, er, oo* (as in "book"), *Yy, a* (schwa), *Pp, ay, Vv, Qq, Jj, Xx, or, Zz, a_e, -y* (as in "baby"), *i_e, ou, ow* (as in "cow"), *ch, Ch, ai, igh, o_e, ir, aw, ew, u_e, ow* (as in "snow"), *ge, ci, ce, kn, ph, oa, oi, ea* (as in "bread")

Cumulative Affixes and Morphographs

Review • *-ed, -en, -er, -es, -est, -ing, -ly, -s, -y, -tion, re-, un-, ex-, -ful, bi-, de-, -able*

★New Letter Sounds, Combinations, Affixes and Morphographs

The Letter Sounds, Combinations, Affixes and Morphographs listed above are reviewed throughout Unit 47.

★New Pattern Words

beach, board, burn, calm, calmly, chance, class, coast, cord, crowd, die, glue, grape, gulp, gulped, heel, it'll, join, lean, leaned, peer, peered, pow, puff, puffed, ribs, scrap, scrape, screech, screechy, screen, sense, shreds, soft, split, spun, squeal, squealed, sting, stove, stretch, stretched, Sue, wood, zip

Known Pattern Words With Affixes* • *appeared, brains, chewed, circles, coins, dented, eats, excitement, fatter, filled, finds, finishes, flashed, floated, groaned, hurrying, knobby, louder, moaned, noises, phones, pointed, points, problems, pushed, rusted, sides, sounded, sticking, talking, voices, walks, whooshed, wrapped, zipped, zoomed*

★New Compound Words

airlock, airlock's, anymore, anyway, classmates, grapefruit, jellyfish, lifeboat, nobody, spacecraft, tiptoe, underside

**Known Pattern Words With Affixes* and *Known Tricky Words With Affixes* are root words students have previously read. The words are new in this unit because they have not previously been read with the affix.

★ = New in this unit

Phonics *(continued)*

★Other New Multisyllabic Words

ahead, allowed, announced, arrive, asteroid, asteroids, beside, children, crunching, danger, explode, exploded, explodes, explosion, follow, handle, inflatable, inflate, inflated, nation, octopus, pilot, rescue, responded, robot, shuttle, shuttle's, silence, sneaker, sneakers, station, tentacles, vacation, whispered, window, windows, wrinkle, wrinkly

★New Tricky Words

against, alien, aliens, alien's, Asha, Asha's, caught, couple, echo, echoed, field, fruit, future, judge, love, loved, Maria, Maria's, metal, nervous, nudge, nudged, shove, shoved, taught, they'd, wherever

Known Tricky Word With Affix* • *wondered*

Fluency

Accuracy, Expression, Phrasing, Rate

Comprehension

Comprehension Strategies

Making Connections, Predicting, Identifying, Describing, Demonstrating, Defining, Applying, Explaining, Inferring, Responding, Visualizing, Illustrating, Summarizing, Monitoring Comprehension, Sequencing, Previewing

Story Elements

Title, Who (Main Character, Characters), Where (Setting), Problem, Goal, What, Action, Cause and Effect, Conclusion

Story Vocabulary

★Alien, ★Asteroid, Rescue, ★Rescue Ball, ★Space Station, ★Space Shuttle

Text Structure

Beginning, Middle, End

Expository Elements

Main Idea and Supporting Details (Facts), Topic

Genre

Science Fiction

Lessons

★Small problems can become big problems.

★Stories of the future may one day be true.

Written Response

Sentence Illustration, Sentence Completion, List, Sentence Writing, Sentence Comprehension—Multiple Choice, Summarizing—Story Map and Written Retell, Paragraph Comprehension, Conventions—Beginning Capital, Period

Skill-Related Vocabulary

Compound Words, Multisyllabic Words, Opposites

Study Skills

Defining Words, Using a Glossary, Using Graphic Organizers (Main Character, Main Idea and Supporting Details), Reading for Purpose, Alphabetical Order, Locating Information

Daily Lesson Planning

ASSESSMENT

Upon completion of this unit, assess each student and proceed to Unit 48 as appropriate. See Making Decisions, page 61, for additional information.

DAILY LESSON FORMAT

BEFORE READING	READING	AFTER READING
Exercises 15–20 minutes	**Storybook Reading** 15–20 minutes	**Partner Reading** 5–10 minutes **Comprehension and Skill Activities** 15–20 minutes

SAMPLE LESSON PLANS

The sample lesson plans illustrate how materials can be used for students with different learning needs. Each lesson plan is designed to provide daily decoding practice and story reading.

6-DAY PLAN		
Day 1 • Exercise 1 • Story 1 • Comprehension and Skill Activity 1* • Homework 1*	**Day 2** • Exercise 2 • Story 2 • Comprehension and Skill Activities 2–3* • Homework 2*	**Day 3** • Exercise 3 • Story 3 • Comprehension and Skill Activities 4–5* • Homework 3*
Day 4 • Exercise 4 • Story 4 • Comprehension and Skill Activities 6–7* • Homework 4*	**Day 5** • Exercise 5 • Story 5 • Comprehension and Skill Activities 8–9* • Homework 5*	**Day 6** • Exercise 6 • Story 6 • Story Summary (*optional*) • Comprehension and Skill Activities 10–11* • Homework 6*

* From *Read Well Plus* Comprehension and Skill Activities (workbook), *Read Well Plus* Homework (blackline masters), or Extra Practice in this book.

8-DAY PLAN • *Pre-Intervention*			
Day 1 • Exercise 1 • Story 1 • Comprehension and Skill Activity 1* • Homework 1*	**Day 2** • Exercise 2 • Story 2 • Comprehension and Skill Activities 2–3* • Homework 2*	**Day 3** • Exercise 3 • Story 3 • Comprehension and Skill Activities 4–5* • Homework 3*	**Day 4** • Exercise 4 • Story 4 • Comprehension and Skill Activities 6–7* • Homework 4*
Day 5 • Exercise 5 • Story 5 • Comprehension and Skill Activities 8–9* • Homework 5*	**Day 6** • Exercise 6 • Story 6 • Story Summary • Comprehension and Skill Activity 10* • Homework 6*	**Day 7** • Review Exercise 6 • Reread Selected Story Passages • Comprehension and Skill Activity 11*	**Day 8** • Extra Practice 1 • Extra Practice 1 Fluency Passage* • Homework: Extra Practice 1 Fluency Passage

PRE-INTERVENTION AND INTERVENTION

See *Getting Started: A Guide to Implementation* for information on how to achieve mastery at a faster pace with students who require eight or more days of instruction.

10-DAY PLAN • *Intervention*				
Day 1 • Exercise 1 • Story 1 • Comprehension and Skill Activity 1* • Homework 1*	**Day 2** • Exercise 2 • Story 2 • Comprehension and Skill Activities 2–3* • Homework 2*	**Day 3** • Exercise 3 • Story 3 • Comprehension and Skill Activities 4–5* • Homework 3*	**Day 4** • Exercise 4 • Story 4 • Comprehension and Skill Activities 6–7* • Homework 4*	**Day 5** • Exercise 5 • Story 5 • Comprehension and Skill Activities 8–9* • Homework 5*
Day 6 • Exercise 6 • Story 6 • Story Summary • Comprehension and Skill Activity 10* • Homework 6*	**Day 7** • Review Exercise 6 • Reread Selected Story Passages • Comprehension and Skill Activity 11*	**Day 8** • Extra Practice 1 • Extra Practice 1 Fluency Passage* • Optional: Have students copy and illustrate sentences from Extra Practice 1. • Homework: Extra Practice 1 Fluency Passage	**Day 9** • Extra Practice 2 • Extra Practice 2 Fluency Passages* • Optional: Have students copy and illustrate sentences from Extra Practice 2. • Homework: Extra Practice 2 Fluency Passages	**Day 10** • Extra Practice 3 • Extra Practice 3 Fluency Passage* • Optional: Have students copy and illustrate sentences from Extra Practice 3. • Homework: Extra Practice 3 Fluency Passage

Materials and Materials Preparation

Core Lessons

Teacher Materials

***READ WELL PLUS* MATERIALS**

- Unit 47 Teacher's Guide
- Sound Cards and Tricky Word Cards for Units 39–47
  (See *Getting Started* for Tricky Word Card Blackline Masters.)

SCHOOL SUPPLIES

- Stopwatch or watch with a second hand

Make one copy per student of each blackline master as appropriate for the group.

Note: For new or difficult Comprehension and Skill Work activities, make overhead transparencies from the blackline masters. Use the transparencies to demonstrate and guide practice.

Student Materials

***READ WELL PLUS* MATERIALS**

- *Read Well Plus* Exercise Book for each student
- Unit 47 Storybook for each student
- Unit 47 Comprehension and Skill Activities for each student (My Activity Book 5)
- Unit 47 Certificate of Achievement (blackline master page 63)
- Unit 47 Homework for each student (blackline masters)
  See *Getting Started* for suggested homework routines.

SCHOOL SUPPLIES

- Pencils, colors (optional—markers, crayons, or colored pencils)

Extra Practice Lessons

Note: Use these lessons only if needed.

Student Materials

***READ WELL PLUS* MATERIALS**

- Unit 47 Extra Practice 1, 2, and 3 Fluency Passages for each student (blackline masters pages 65, 67, and 68)

SCHOOL SUPPLIES

- Pencils, colors (markers, crayons, or colored pencils)
- White boards or paper

How to Teach the Lessons

Teach from this section. Each instructional component is outlined in an easy-to-teach format. Special tips are provided to help you nurture student progress.

Exercise 1

- Storybook Introduction
- Story 1
- Comprehension and Skill Activity 1

Exercise 2

- Story 2
- Comprehension and Skill Activities 2–3

Exercise 3

- Story 3
- Comprehension and Skill Activities 4–5

Exercise 4

- Story 4
- Comprehension and Skill Activities 6–7

Exercise 5

- Story 5
- Comprehension and Skill Activities 8–9

Exercise 6

- Story 6
- Story Summary (*optional*)
- Comprehension and Skill Activities 10–11

BUILDING INDEPENDENCE

Next Steps • Principles of Instruction

For Units 39–50, follow the scaffolded principles of instruction below.

Provide demonstration and/or guided practice only with:
- New sounds
- New Tricky Words
- New multisyllabic words

Provide independent practice (practice without your assistance or voice) on:
- New and review pattern words with known sounds
- Review Tricky Words
- Review multisyllabic words
- All words and sounds prior to completing the Exercise

If students make errors, provide appropriate corrections.
- Have students identify any difficult sound and then sound out the word. Provide discrimination practice.
- Reintroduce difficult Tricky Words based on the initial introduction procedures.

If students require your assistance on words with known sounds, evaluate placement and consider a Jell-Well Review.

1 SOUND REVIEW

Use the Sound Cards for Units 39–46 and selected Review Sound Cards and Tricky Word Cards.

2 SOUND AND SENTENCE PRACTICE

- Have students read the first sentence, then identify the words with /u_e/ as in "blue."
- Repeat with the remaining sentence and the corresponding sound /ur/ as in "turn."
- Provide repeated practice to build fluency. Mix group and individual turns.

★ 3 ACCURACY AND FLUENCY BUILDING

- For tasks A through E, have students read any underlined part and then each word.
- Provide repeated practice, building accuracy first, then fluency on each task and column.

Note: Specific instructions and sample scripts for new and difficult tasks appear below.

B2. Affix Practice

- Have students identify the affix /-tion/.
- For each word, have students read the affix, then the whole word.
- Repeat practice. Mix group and individual turns, independent of your voice.

C1 and D1. Multisyllabic Words

- For the list of words divided by syllables, have students read each syllable out loud and finger count how many syllables are in the word.
  Use the word in a sentence as appropriate.

  Note: If you provide a sentence stem for Multisyllabic Words or Tricky Words, and you anticipate your students will be able to read the word without your assistance, then do not read the word with them.

tiptoe	2 syllables	He was trying to be quiet. He was walking on . . . *tiptoe.*
airlock	2 syllables	A room or place where air cannot escape is called an . . . *airlock.*
backpack	2 syllables	[Lindsey] carries [her] schoolwork in a . . . (*backpack*).
classmates	2 syllables	The other students in your class are your . . . (*classmates*).
nobody	3 syllables	I thought someone was at the door, but *nobody* was there.
asteroids	3 syllables	Big chunks of rock that orbit in space are . . . *asteroids.*
excite	2 syllables	The circus is so interesting and thrilling, it will . . . *excite* you.
excited	3 syllables	She was really looking forward to the field trip. She was . . . (*excited*).
excitement	3 syllables	Her laughs and smiles showed her . . . *excitement.*

- For the list of whole words, build accuracy and then fluency. Repeat, mixing group and individual turns.

Note: The light scripting in *Read Well* will help you visualize instruction as you prepare for a lesson. Scripting provides an instructional guide and is not intended to be memorized or read to students.

(*continued*)

Unit 47 Exercise 1

For use with Story 1

1. SOUND REVIEW Use the Sound Cards for Units 39–46 and selected Review Cards.

2. SOUND AND SENTENCE PRACTICE Have students read each sentence, then identify the words with underlined sounds. Next, read the underlined sounds.

I'll give you a clue why the glue is blue. Just look at Sue!
Turn off the stove so you don't get hurt. You don't want to burn your fingers.

★3. ACCURACY/FLUENCY BUILDING For each section, have students read any underlined part, then read each word. Next, have students read the whole column and identify what's the same about each word. ADVANCED ACCURACY/FLUENCY Have students read the word first, then read the underlined sound.

A1 Sound Practice	B1 Word Endings	C1 Multisyllabic Words	D1 Multisyllabic Words	E1 Contractions
voices	squealed	tip-toe	ex-cite	it will
noises	leaned	air-lock	ex-cit-ed	it'll
points	appeared	back-pack	ex-cite-ment	**E2** Tricky Words
road	sounded	class-mates	excite	★Asha
toad	dented	no-bod-y	excited	★Maria
boat	hurrying	as-ter-oids	excitement	wonder
since	**B2** Affix Practice	tiptoe	**D2** Sound Review	★wondered
notice	-tion	airlock	crowded	★echo
A2 Sound Review	fiction	backpack	allowed	★echoed
flashed	sta-tion	classmates	rusted	★love
phones	station	nobody	whispered	★loved
shuttle	in-tro-duc-tion	asteroids		
children	introduction			

★4. TRICKY WORDS IN CONTEXT See the Teacher's Guide.

To people from Earth, living things who are not from Earth would be aliens. ★ aliens
You will grow up and become an adult in the future. ★ future
Large buildings are made out of wood, brick, or metal. ★ metal
The kids play baseball in the field next to their school. ★ field

★5. TRICKY WORD FAMILY See the Teacher's Guide.

★caught ★taught

6. DAILY STORY READING

49

FOR ENGLISH LANGUAGE LEARNERS AND CHILDREN WITH LANGUAGE DELAYS

Watch for the ◆◆s. Provide repeated use of the oral language patterns within and outside of lessons to build language and vocabulary.

MR. Z's TEAM EXPECTATIONS

Provide a quick review of expectations before starting the lesson.

1. Sit up.
2. Follow directions.
3. Help each other.
4. Work hard and have fun.

◆◆ SENTENCE SUGGESTIONS

(A1) since—It has been a long time *since* we've seen each other.

(A2) flashed—The lightning *flashed* in the sky.

Sentence Suggestions: Use sentences *after* decoding the individual word. Using sentences emphasizes that words have meaning.

E2. Tricky Words

★ **New Tricky Words: Asha, Maria, wondered, echo, echoed, love, loved**

- For each new Tricky Word, have students identify known parts of the word. Use the word in a sentence, or tell students the word as appropriate.

  Asha (Aw-shuh)
  Look at the first word. The word is "Asha."
  One of the characters in our new story is . . . *Asha.*
  Say the word five times. (Asha, Asha, Asha, Asha, Asha)

Maria	Another character in our new story is . . . *Maria.*
wondered	We *wondered* why they were late.
echo	When you say the same thing after me, you are my . . . *echo.*
echoed	"Where is she?" [Sara] asked. "Where is she?" [Jared] . . . *echoed.*
love	I *love* my family.
loved	Nate has always *loved* his dog.

- Have students read the words, building accuracy, then fluency. Repeat, mixing group and individual turns, independent of your voice.

★ 4 TRICKY WORDS IN CONTEXT

- Tell students the underlined word is a new Tricky Word. Remind students to use the sounds they know and the sentence to figure out how to say the word. Assist as needed. Have students read the individual word.
- For the list of Tricky Words, build accuracy and then fluency. Repeat, mixing group and individual turns.

★ 5 TRICKY WORD FAMILY

- Introduce the word "caught" and use it in a sentence.
  The first word is "caught." I went fishing with my dad and *caught* a fish.
  Tell me the word. (caught)
- Introduce the rhyming word "taught."
  The next word rhymes with "caught."
  Tell me the word. (taught)
  [Mr. Jimenez] *taught* you how to [jump rope].
- Repeat practice, mixing group and individual turns, independent of your voice.

6 DAILY STORY READING—See Daily Lesson Planning.

7 COMPREHENSION AND SKILL ACTIVITY—See Daily Lesson Planning.

Note: The light scripting in *Read Well* will help you visualize instruction as you prepare for a lesson. Scripting provides an instructional guide and is not intended to be memorized or read to students.

Unit 47 Exercise 1

For use with Story 1

1. SOUND REVIEW Use the Sound Cards for Units 39–46 and selected Review Cards.

2. SOUND AND SENTENCE PRACTICE Have students read each sentence, then identify the words with underlined sounds. Next, read the underlined sounds.

> I'll give you a clue why the glue is blue. Just look at Sue!
> Turn off the stove so you don't get hurt. You don't want to burn your fingers.

★3. ACCURACY/FLUENCY BUILDING For each section, have students read any underlined part, then read each word. Next, have students read the whole column and identify what's the same about each word. ADVANCED ACCURACY/FLUENCY Have students read the word first, then read the underlined sound.

A1 Sound Practice	B1 Word Endings	C1 Multisyllabic Words	D1 Multisyllabic Words	E1 Contractions
voices	squealed	tip-toe	ex-cite	it will
noises	leaned	air-lock	ex-cit-ed	it'll
points	appeared	back-pack	ex-cite-ment	**E2** Tricky Words
road	sounded	class-mates	excite	★Asha
toad	dented	no-bod-y	excited	★Maria
boat	hurrying	as-ter-oids	excitement	wonder
since	**B2** Affix Practice	tiptoe	**D2** Sound Review	★wondered
notice	-tion	airlock	crowded	★echo
A2 Sound Review	fiction	backpack	allowed	★echoed
flashed	sta-tion	classmates	rusted	★love
phones	station	nobody	whispered	★loved
shuttle	in-tro-duc-tion	asteroids		
children	introduction			

★4. TRICKY WORDS IN CONTEXT See the Teacher's Guide.

To people from Earth, living things who are not from Earth would be aliens.	★ aliens
You will grow up and become an adult in the future.	★ future
Large buildings are made out of wood, brick, or metal.	★ metal
The kids play baseball in the field next to their school.	★ field

★5. TRICKY WORD FAMILY See the Teacher's Guide.

★caught ★taught

6. DAILY STORY READING

49

❶ INTRODUCING THE STORYBOOK AND TABLE OF CONTENTS

Identifying—Title, Making Connections

Have students read the storybook title—*Space.*

On a clear night, if you look out at the stars, you are looking into space.

Raise your hand if you would like to travel into space.

Predicting

Have students turn to the Table of Contents on page 2.

Turn to the Table of Contents on page 2. What is this unit about?

(A space school)

Do you think it would be fun to go to school in space?

What do you think it would be like?

Read the story title and chapter titles. Do you think the story will be fact or fiction? What makes you think it's fiction?

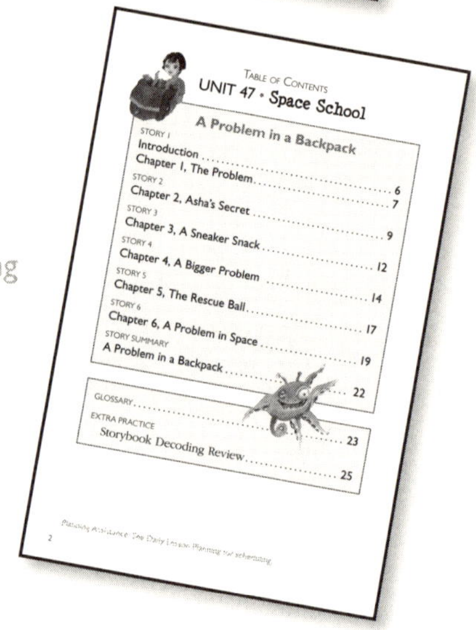
Table of Contents
UNIT 47 • Space School
A Problem in a Backpack
STORY 1
Introduction 6
Chapter 1, The Problem 7
STORY 2
Chapter 2, Asha's Secret 9
STORY 3
Chapter 3, A Sneaker Snack 12
STORY 4
Chapter 4, A Bigger Problem 14
STORY 5
Chapter 5, The Rescue Ball 17
STORY 6
Chapter 6, A Problem in Space 19
STORY SUMMARY
A Problem in a Backpack 22
GLOSSARY 23
EXTRA PRACTICE
Storybook Decoding Review 25

❷ INTRODUCING VOCABULARY

Vocabulary—alien, asteroid, rescue ball, space shuttle, space station

alien

The first word is "alien." Read the word. (alien)

Let's read the definition together. An *alien* is a living thing that is not from around here. To people on Earth, an alien would be a living thing that is not from Earth.

asteroid

The next word is "asteroid." Read the word. (asteroid)

Let's read the definition together. An *asteroid* is a rock in space that circles the Sun.

rescue ball

Read the next word. (rescue ball)

A *rescue ball* is an inflatable ball that can hold air and a person in an emergency. A rescue ball is like a space lifeboat.

This story must have a rescue in it. Let's see if we can make predictions. Who do you think will need a rescue? How will that character be rescued?

space shuttle

Read the next word. (space shuttle)

A *space shuttle* is a spacecraft that moves people and things around in space.

space station

Read the next word. (space station)

A *space station* is a spacecraft that can stay in space for a long time. People can live in a space station.

❸ DEFINING VOCABULARY

Vocabulary—rescue

rescue

Let's see if we can define the word "rescue." Start with "A *rescue* is when someone is . . ." Now let's look "rescue" up in the glossary. Turn to page 23.

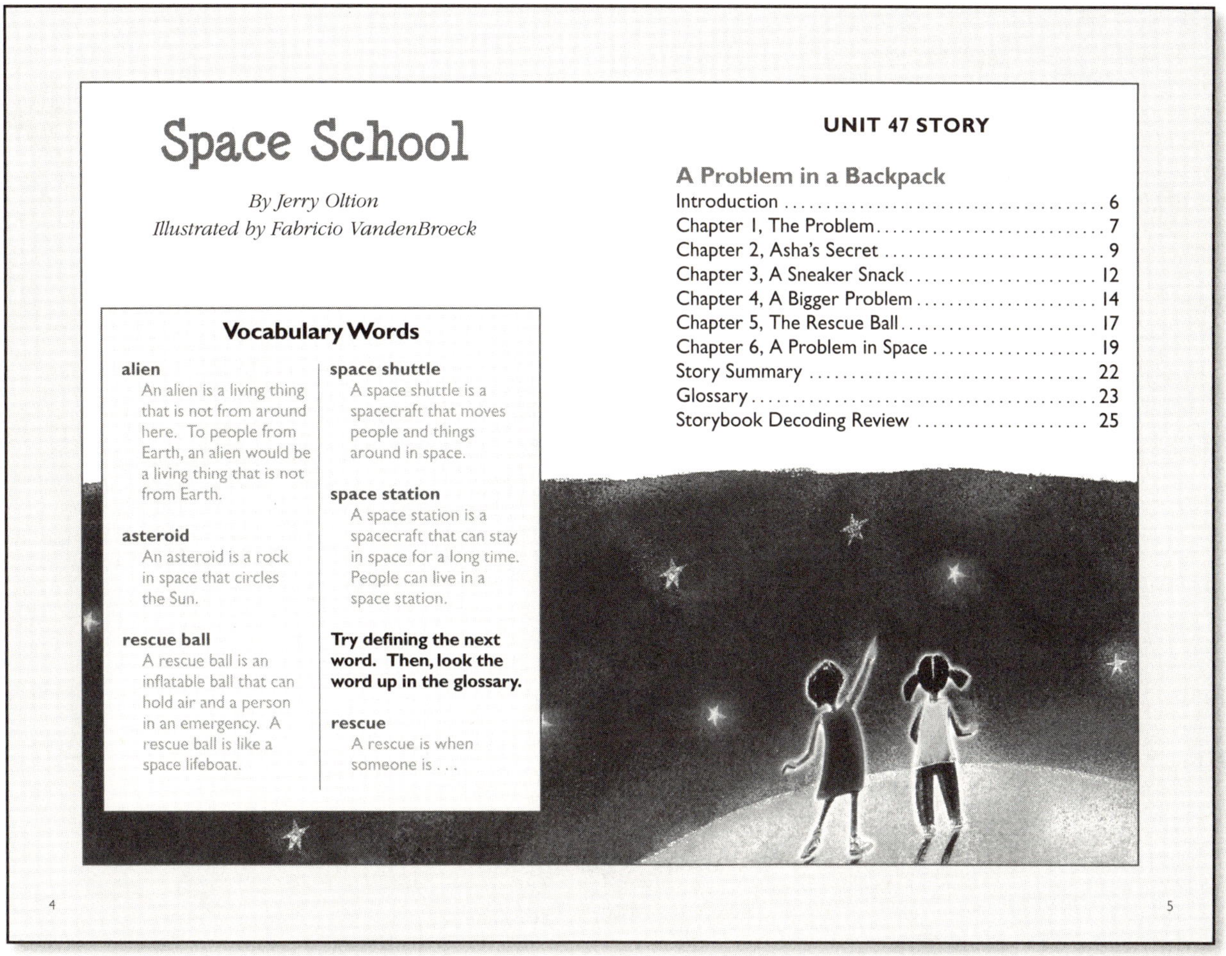

Space School

By Jerry Oltion
Illustrated by Fabricio VandenBroeck

Vocabulary Words

alien
An alien is a living thing that is not from around here. To people from Earth, an alien would be a living thing that is not from Earth.

asteroid
An asteroid is a rock in space that circles the Sun.

rescue ball
A rescue ball is an inflatable ball that can hold air and a person in an emergency. A rescue ball is like a space lifeboat.

space shuttle
A space shuttle is a spacecraft that moves people and things around in space.

space station
A space station is a spacecraft that can stay in space for a long time. People can live in a space station.

Try defining the next word. Then, look the word up in the glossary.

rescue
A rescue is when someone is . . .

4

UNIT 47 STORY

A Problem in a Backpack

5

Vocabulary Words

alien
An alien is a living thing that is not from around here. To people from Earth, an alien would be a living thing that is not from Earth.

asteroid
An asteroid is a rock in space that circles the Sun.

rescue ball
A rescue ball is an inflatable ball that can hold air and a person in an emergency. A rescue ball is like a space lifeboat.

space shuttle
A space shuttle is a spacecraft that moves people and things around in space.

space station
A space station is a spacecraft that can stay in space for a long time. People can live in a space station.

Try defining the next word. Then, look the word up in the glossary.

rescue
A rescue is when someone is . . .

Defining Vocabulary—Alien, Asteroid, Rescue Ball, Space Shuttle, Space Station, Rescue

COMPREHENSION BUILDING: DISCUSSION QUESTIONS AND TEACHER THINK ALOUDS

- Ask questions and discuss text on the *first* reading.
- If students have difficulty with a question, think aloud with them or reread the portion of the story that answers the question. Then ask the question again.

PROCEDURES

1. Introduction

Have students read the title of the story. Say something like: If you've ever had a problem, put your hand on your head. How did the problem make you feel?
The problem in this story is a little different.

2. First Reading

- Mix group and individual turns, independent of your voice. Have students work toward an accuracy goal of 0–2 errors. Gently correct and quietly keep track of errors made by all students in the group.
- After reading the story, practice any difficult words.

3. Optional Second Reading

If the group has not reached the accuracy goal or is reading dysfluently, have the group reread the story, mixing group and individual turns.

4. Repeated Readings

a. Short Passage Practice

Select short passages from the story. Demonstrate expressive, fluent reading. Guide practice with your voice. Then provide individual turns.

b. Partner Reading

5. Homework 1

STORY 1

A Problem in a Backpack

Look at the picture. Predict what the story will be about.[1]

INTRODUCTION

If you look into the sky as far as you can see, you are looking out into space. Since the beginning of time, people have looked into space and wondered what is out there.

This story is about children who live and go to school in space. It takes place in the future. Is the story fact or fiction?

6

1 **Inferring, Predicting** (The story will be about two kids, space, and a problem in a backpack.)

CHAPTER 1
The Problem

Maria stood on tiptoe to see over the heads of her classmates. They were all standing in line at the space station's airlock, waiting for a shuttle. They were going to take a field trip to the asteroid mine. Maria was waiting for her friend Asha. Where could she be? Asha loved asteroids. She wouldn't miss this field trip for anything!

FINGER TRACKING
Reminder
To maintain attention and build fluency, continue having students track text with their fingers. Give turns to individual students who are following along.

The hall echoed with voices as the other kids talked about the shuttle ride. Everyone was excited. Maria wondered if the teacher would let her call Asha to ask where she was. Maria was just going to ask when Asha came hurrying up with her backpack in her hands.

"You're late!" Maria said. "We're about to leave."

Asha smiled, leaned close, and whispered in Maria's ear. "I had a little problem. In fact, I still have it!" Then, Asha giggled.

Where do the children live?1 Who are the main characters?2 Where is the class going?3 What is an asteroid?4

How do you feel when you have a problem?5 Let's read the last paragraph again. As you read, listen for a clue about Asha's problem.6

Asha seems happy about having a problem. In the next chapter, you'll find out three things—what the problem was, why Asha was happy about her problem, and something funny about the teacher.7

1. **Identifying—Where** (The children live on a space station.)
2. **Identifying—Who (Main Characters)** (The main characters are Maria and Asha.)
3. **Identifying—Where** (The class is going on a field trip to the asteroid mine.)
4. **Defining Vocabulary—Asteroid** (An asteroid is a rock that circles the Sun.)
5. **Making Connections, Describing**
6. **Reading for Purpose**
7. **Teacher Think Aloud, Previewing**

Note: Questions focus students on important story elements and provide prompts for story discussions. Answers provide guidance, not verbatim responses.

STORY COMPREHENSION

Make an overhead from the blackline master to guide practice as needed.

BUILDING INDEPENDENCE
Principles of Instruction

For each step, demonstrate and guide practice only as needed.

- **Demonstrate**: Have students orally answer the items while you demonstrate how to complete the page.
- **Guide**: Have students orally answer the items, but do not demonstrate how to complete the page.
- **Independent With Support**: Have students silently read over the items and ask any questions they may have.

Making Connections

Describing
Complete Sentence,
Conventions—Beginning Capital, Period

Identifying—Main Characters

Identifying—Where

Identifying—Where, Inferring

Locating Information
Defining Vocabulary—Rescue
Complete Sentence,
Conventions—Beginning Capital, Period

Predicting
Conventions—Period

COMPREHENSION AND SKILL
Unit 47 Activity 1
For use after Exercise 1 and Story 1

Name ____________________

Story Comprehension
Chapter 1, The Problem

1 **Have you ever been on a field trip?** ● yes ○ no

2 **Describe your favorite field trip.** (What is item 2 about? It's about your favorite field trip, so start your answer with *My favorite field trip was . . .*)
(Accept any reasonable response.)
My favorite field trip was the zoo.

3 **Who are the main characters in this story?**
○ two amphibians—Asha and Maria
○ two detectives—Asha and Maria
● two friends—Asha and Maria

4 **Where is the class going?**
○ on a field trip to a zoo
○ on a field trip to a park
● on a field trip to an asteroid mine

5 **Where do you think Asha's problem is?**
● in her backpack ○ at home ○ in the refrigerator

★6 **Look in the glossary. Find the word "rescue." Copy the definition.**
A rescue is when someone is saved from danger.

7 **What do you predict will happen in "A Problem in a Backpack"?**
(Accept any reasonable response.)
I predict that something funny will happen.

 97

PROCEDURES

For each step, demonstrate and guide practice as needed.

1. Multiple Choice—Basic Instructions (Items 1, 3–5)
Have students fill in the bubble for the correct answer.

2. Sentence Writing—Basic Instructions (Item 2)
- Have students read the question and brainstorm possible responses.
- Have students write a complete sentence that starts with a capital letter and ends with a period.

★ **3. Using a Glossary, Copying a Definition—Basic Instructions** (Item 6)
Have students look in the glossary, find the word "rescue," and copy the definition. Have them copy the complete definition, starting with a capital letter and ending with a period.

4. Sentence Completion—Basic Instructions (Item 7)
Have students read and complete the sentence and place a period at the end.

Note: For each Comprehension and Skill Activity, correct completed work. For difficult items, think aloud with students. Say things like: "I'm not sure about the answer. Let's look in our books." "Does the first answer make sense?" "Is the answer completely correct?"

❶ SOUND REVIEW

Use the Sound Cards from Units 39–47 and selected Review Sound Cards and Tricky Word Cards.

❷ SOUND AND SENTENCE PRACTICE

- Have students read the first sentence, then identify the words with /ur/ as in "turn."
- Repeat with the remaining sentence and the corresponding sound /u_e/ as in "blue."
- Provide repeated practice to build fluency. Mix group and individual turns.

❸ ACCURACY AND FLUENCY BUILDING

Provide repeated practice, building accuracy first, then fluency.
Note: For advanced practice, have students read the word, then any underlined part.

B1 and C1. Multisyllabic Words

- For the list of words divided by syllables, have students read each syllable out loud and finger count how many syllables are in the word.
  Use the word in a sentence as appropriate.

appeared	2 syllables	Asha *appeared* to be excited.
sounded	2 syllables	When I came home late, my dad *sounded* worried.
dented	2 syllables	When he bumped his car into the tree, it got . . . *dented.*
crowded	2 syllables	We couldn't sit on the shuttle. The seats were too . . . *crowded.*
allowed	2 syllables	Adults can see the movie. Children aren't . . . *allowed.*
whispered	2 syllables	Asha wanted only Maria to hear, so she . . . *whispered.*
station	2 syllables	Our class went on a trip to the fire . . . *station.*
hurrying	3 syllables	I'll be ready in a minute. I am . . . *hurrying.*
nobody	3 syllables	I thought someone was at the door, but . . . *nobody* was there.
excited	3 syllables	She was really looking forward to the field trip. She was . . . *(excited).*
excitement	3 syllables	Her laughs and smiles showed her . . . *excitement.*
asteroids	3 syllables	Big chunks of rock that orbit the Sun are . . . *asteroids.*

- For the list of whole words, build accuracy and then fluency. Repeat, mixing group and individual turns.

❹ TRICKY WORDS IN CONTEXT

- Tell students the underlined word is a Tricky Word. Remind students to use the sounds they know and the sentence to figure out how to say the word. Assist as needed. Have students read the individual word.
- For the list of Tricky Words, build accuracy and then fluency. Repeat, mixing group and individual turns.

❺ TRICKY WORD FAMILY

Have students read the words "caught" and "taught," then identify that they are rhyming words. Use each word in a sentence.

❻ DAILY STORY READING—See Daily Lesson Planning.

❼ COMPREHENSION AND SKILL ACTIVITIES—See Daily Lesson Planning.

Unit 47 Exercise 2
For use with Story 2 as needed

1. SOUND REVIEW Use the Sound Cards for Units 39–47 and selected Review Cards.

2. SOUND AND SENTENCE PRACTICE Have students read each sentence, then identify the words with underlined sounds. Next, read the underlined sounds.

> Turn off the stove so you don't get hurt. You don't want to burn your fingers.
> I'll give you a clue why the glue is blue. Just look at Sue!

3. ACCURACY/FLUENCY BUILDING For each section, have students read any underlined part, then read each word. Next, have students read the whole column and identify what's the same about each word. ADVANCED ACCURACY/FLUENCY Have students read the word first, then read the underlined sound.

A1 Sound Practice	B1 Multisyllabic Words	C1 Multisyllabic Words	D1 Contractions
boat	ap-peared	sta-tion	you're
toad	sound-ed	hur-ry-ing	we're
road	dent-ed	no-bod-y	it'll
voices	crowd-ed	ex-cit-ed	**D2 Tricky Words**
points	al-lowed	ex-cite-ment	aliens
noises	whis-pered	as-ter-oids	Asha
A2 Sound Review	appeared	station	echoed
leaned	sounded	hurrying	field
squealed	dented	nobody	future
classmates	crowded	excited	loved
tiptoe	allowed	excitement	Maria
airlock	whispered	asteroids	metal
backpack			wondered

4. TRICKY WORDS IN CONTEXT See the Teacher's Guide.

The hall echoed with voices.	echoed
Asha loved asteroids.	loved
Since the beginning of time, people have looked into space and wondered what is out there.	wondered

5. TRICKY WORD FAMILY See the Teacher's Guide.

caught taught

6. DAILY STORY READING

50

ACKNOWLEDGING DESIRED BEHAVIORS

Make a special effort to notice and congratulate the least mature students whenever they are taking steps toward greater cooperation, responsibility, and independence. Say something like: [Cecilia], your finger was on the right word when it was [Miguel's] turn. You get to read the next word.

◆◆ SENTENCE SUGGESTIONS

(**D2**) aliens—Living things that are not from Earth are . . . *aliens.*

(**D2**) metal—Large buildings are made out of wood, brick, or . . . *metal.*

Sentence Suggestions: Use sentences *after* decoding the individual word. Using sentences emphasizes that words have meaning.

◆◆ Repeat and extend practice for English Language Learners and students with language delays.

PROCEDURES

1. Introduction

Have students summarize Chapter 1 by following the gray text in the storybook.

2. First and Second Reading

- Have students whisper read Chapter 2.
- Have students read Chapter 2 out loud. Mix group and individual turns.

  Have students word toward an accuracy goal of 0–2 errors.

  Quietly keep track of errors made by all students in the group.

  Gently correct any errors and have students reread the sentence.
- After reading the story, practice any difficult words.

3. Repeated Readings

a. Timed Readings

As time allows, have students do Timed Readings while others follow along.

b. Partner Reading

During students' daily independent work, have them do Partner Reading.

4. Homework 2

Have students read the story at home. (*Read Well Plus* Homework is available in blackline masters.)

CHAPTER 2

Asha's Secret

What happened in Chapter 1?[1] Can you predict what Asha's secret is?[2]

Asha was late to school on the day of the big field trip. Asha had told Maria that she was late because of a problem, but Asha had sounded excited. From her voice, Maria knew Asha wasn't in trouble. What else could she mean? Maria asked, "Why are you so happy about a problem?"

"Because nobody has ever caught one before," Asha said.

"Caught one? How could you catch a problem? Unless . . . "

1 **Summarizing** (Asha and Maria's class was going on a field trip to an asteroid mine. Asha was late. When Asha arrived, she told Maria that she had a problem.)

2 **Predicting, Monitoring Comprehension, Teacher Think Aloud**
We may not have enough information to predict what the secret is. What do we know so far? (We know that Asha whispered and giggled when she talked to Maria about a problem.) So, all we know is that it must not be a bad problem. She wasn't upset. I wonder what the secret is.

STORY 2

Asha could only mean one thing. Small aliens had appeared on the space station a few weeks ago. Nobody knew where they had come from, but the little animals were getting into everything.

"You caught a problem?" Maria asked.

Asha flashed a big smile and grinned.

Maria squealed. "Really? Can I see it?"

"Keep your voice down!" Asha whispered. "If the teacher finds out, it'll take it away."

Maria looked around. There were fifty kids and only one teacher. Their teacher was an old worn-out model. Its metal body was dented and rusted with age.

It was too busy getting the kids ready for the field trip to notice Maria and Asha's excitement.

Look at the picture. Why did Maria call her teacher "it" instead of "he" or "she"?[1] Describe the teacher.[2]

10

❶ **Teacher Think Aloud, Inferring**
People are called "he" or "she." Things are called "it." Is the teacher a person? (No)

❷ **Describing** (The teacher isn't a person. The teacher is a robot!)

FOCUS ON DESCRIPTION

After completing the page, say something like:
Let's go back and reread the description of the teacher. Find the next to the last paragraph. It begins, "Maria looked around. There were fifty kids . . ." (Maria looked around. There were fifty kids and only one teacher. Their teacher was an old worn-out model. Its metal body was dented and rusted with age.)

EXPLAINING, MAKING CONNECTIONS, RESPONDING

I think that's funny—having a robot for a teacher. Raise your hand if you think it would be fun to have a robot for a teacher.
Why do you think it would be fun?

STORY COMPREHENSION

Make an overhead from the blackline master to guide practice as needed.

COMPREHENSION AND SKILL

Unit 47 Activity 2
For use after Exercise 2 and Story 2

Name ____________________

Story Comprehension

Chapter 2, Asha's Secret

Identifying—What
Complete Sentence,
Conventions—Beginning Capital, Period

1 **What was in Asha's backpack?** (What is item 1 about? It's about what was in the backpack. A problem was in the backpack, so start your answer with *A problem was* . . .)

A problem was in Asha's backpack.

Identifying—What

2 **A funny thing happened in this chapter. We found out that . . .**

- ● the teacher was a robot.
- ○ the kids were on a field trip.

Describing
Complete Sentence,
Conventions—Beginning Capital, Period

3 **Look at the picture on page 11. Describe the children's teacher.** (Item 3 is about the children's teacher. Think about how you will start your answer. Start with *The children's teacher was* . . . Write two sentences about the robot.) (Accept any reasonable response.)

The children's teacher was an old robot. It was dented and rusty.

Identifying—What

4 **What was the problem?**

- ● The problem was an alien—a little animal from someplace in space.
- ○ The problem was an alien—a dinosaur from long ago.
- ○ The problem was false teeth in the backpack.

Visualizing, Illustrating

5 **Think about an alien from space. What do you think a space alien would look like? Draw a picture in the box. Don't peek in your book!**

98 © Sopris West Educational Services. All Rights Reserved.

CHECKOUT OPPORTUNITY

Listen to your students read individually while others work.

PROCEDURES

For each step, demonstrate and guide practice as needed.

1. Sentence Writing—Basic Instructions (Items 1, 3)

- Have students read the question and brainstorm possible responses using complete sentences.
- Have students write complete sentences that start with capital letters and end with periods.

2. Multiple Choice—Basic Instructions (Items 2, 4)

Have students fill in the bubble for the correct answer.

3. Sentence Illustration—Basic Instructions (Item 5)

Have students read each sentence and then complete the illustration.

Note: For each Comprehension and Skill Activity, correct completed work. For difficult items, think aloud with students. Say things like: "I'm not sure about the answer. Let's look in our books." "Does the first answer make sense?" "Is the answer completely correct?"

★ MULTISYLLABIC WORDS AND RHYMING POEM

Identifying—Syllables

Identifying—Rhyming Words

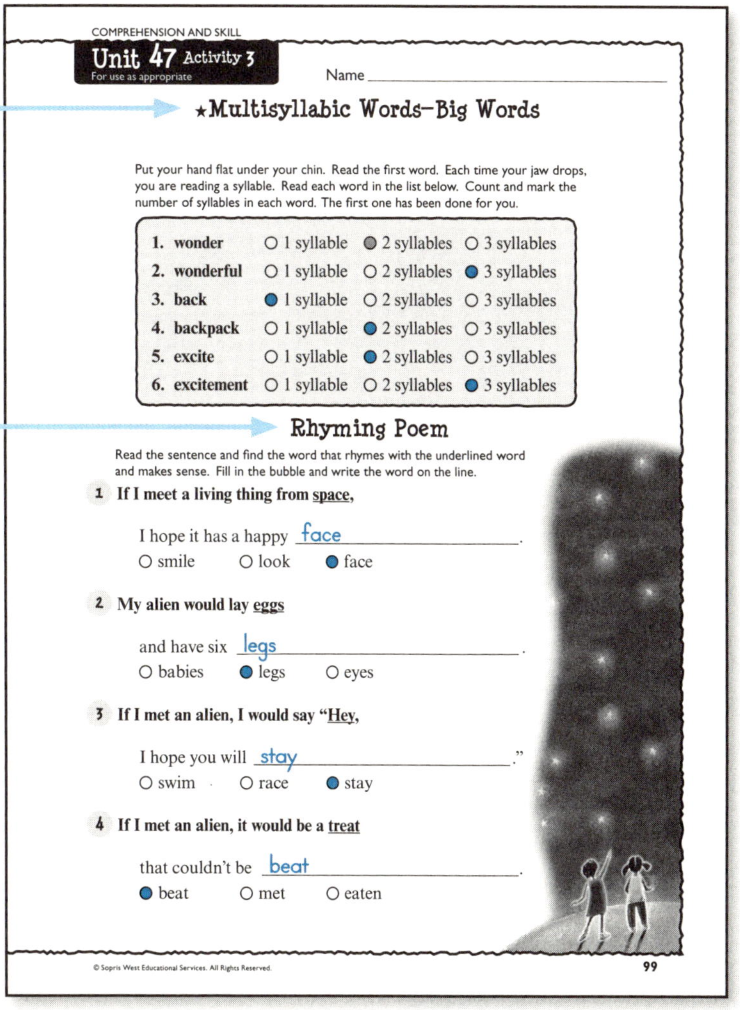
COMPREHENSION AND SKILL

Unit 47 Activity 3

For use as appropriate

Name ______

★Multisyllabic Words–Big Words

Put your hand flat under your chin. Read the first word. Each time your jaw drops, you are reading a syllable. Read each word in the list below. Count and mark the number of syllables in each word. The first one has been done for you.

1. wonder	○ 1 syllable	● 2 syllables	○ 3 syllables
2. wonderful	○ 1 syllable	○ 2 syllables	● 3 syllables
3. back	● 1 syllable	○ 2 syllables	○ 3 syllables
4. backpack	○ 1 syllable	● 2 syllables	○ 3 syllables
5. excite	○ 1 syllable	● 2 syllables	○ 3 syllables
6. excitement	○ 1 syllable	○ 2 syllables	● 3 syllables

Rhyming Poem

Read the sentence and find the word that rhymes with the underlined word and makes sense. Fill in the bubble and write the word on the line.

1 **If I meet a living thing from space,**

I hope it has a happy face.

○ smile ○ look ● face

2 **My alien would lay eggs**

and have six legs.

○ babies ● legs ○ eyes

3 **If I met an alien, I would say "Hey,**

I hope you will stay."

○ swim ○ race ● stay

4 **If I met an alien, it would be a treat**

that couldn't be beat.

● beat ○ met ○ eaten

99

CHECKOUT OPPORTUNITY

Listen to your students read individually while others work.

PROCEDURES

For each step, demonstrate and guide practice as needed.

★ **1. Multisyllabic Words—Introductory Instructions** (Items 1–6)

- Have students put their hands flat under their chins and read the first word.

  Put your hands, palms facing down, under your chins. Say the first word. (wonder) Did you feel your hand move when you said the word? (Yes) Each time your hand moves you are saying a syllable. Syllables are parts of words. Big words or multisyllabic words have more than one syllable. Say the first word again. (wonder)

  Have them count each time their jaws drop.

  How many times did your jaw drop? (Two times) Right, so there are two syllables in the word "wonder."

  Have students fill in the bubble with the correct answer.
- Repeat for items 2–6.

2. Rhyming Poem, Multiple Choice, Sentence Completion—Basic Instructions (Items 1–4)

- Have students read each sentence, and then find the word that rhymes with the underlined word and makes sense.

  Have them fill in the bubble for the correct answer and write the answer in the blank.
- Have students read the whole poem.

❶ SOUND REVIEW

Use the Sound Cards for Units 39–47 and selected Review Sound Cards and Tricky Word Cards.

❷ SOUND AND SENTENCE PRACTICE

- Have students read each sentence, then identify the underlined sounds.
- Repeat sentences to build accuracy and fluency.

❸ ACCURACY AND FLUENCY BUILDING

For each task, provide repeated practice, building accuracy first, then fluency.

D1. Multisyllabic Words

- For the list of words divided by syllables, have students read each syllable out loud and finger count how many syllables are in the word.
  Use the word in a sentence as appropriate.

teacher	2 syllables	When you grow up, would you like to be a . . . *(teacher)?*
fatter	2 syllables	My dog likes to eat so he got . . . *(fatter).*
sneaker	2 syllables	Some people call a tennis shoe a . . . *sneaker.*
shuttle	2 syllables	I would love to ride on a space . . . *shuttle.*
responded	3 syllables	Another way to say "[Jackie] answered" is "[Jackie] . . . *responded."*
tentacles	3 syllables	An octopus has eight long arms called . . . *tentacles.*

- For the list of whole words, build accuracy and then fluency. Repeat, mixing group and individual turns.

E2. Tricky Words

★ **New Tricky Words: shove, shoved, nudge, nudged, fruit, grapefruit**

- For each new Tricky Word, have students identify known parts of the word.
  Use the word in a sentence, or tell students the word as appropriate.

shove

This word is tricky. Sound it out in your head. The sentence will help you figure out how to say the word.

A push is a . . . *(shove).*

Demonstrate shoving the door. This is a . . . *(shove).*

shoved	What did I do? (You *shoved* the door.)
nudge	**Show students a gentle nudge.** I wanted [Greg's] attention so I gave him a . . . *nudge.*
nudged	What did I do? (You *nudged* [Greg].)
fruit	An apple, an orange, and a banana are all . . . *fruit.*
grapefruit	For breakfast, I like . . . *grapefruit.*

- Have students read the words, building accuracy, then fluency. Repeat, mixing group and individual turns, independent of your voice.

(continued)

Unit 47 Exercise 3

For use with Story 3

1. SOUND REVIEW Use the Sound Cards for Units 39–47 and selected Review Cards.

2. SOUND AND SENTENCE PRACTICE Have students read the sentence, then identify the words with underlined sounds. Next, read the underlined sounds.

The alien's knobby knees knock when it walks.
It also makes noise with its huge voice.
Listen to its metal body groan, moan, and croak.

★3. ACCURACY/FLUENCY BUILDING For each section, have students read any underlined part, then read each word. Next, have students read the whole column and identify what's the same about each word. ADVANCED ACCURACY/FLUENCY Have students read the word first, then read the underlined sound.

A1 Sound Practice	B1 Bossy E	C1 Word Endings	D1 Multisyllabic Words	E1 Sound Review
since	sides	wrapped	teach-er	chewed
voice	beside	stretched	fat-ter	pointed
place	grape	gulped	sneak-er	louder
noticed	**B2** Sound Practice	stick	shut-tle	saw
change	bread	sticking	re-spond-ed	**E2** Tricky Words
page	read	crunch	ten-ta-cles	★shove
large	head	crunching	teacher	★shoved
A2 Sound Review	ahead	finish	fatter	★nudge
heel	across	finishes	sneaker	★nudged
ribs	away	wrinkle	shuttle	★fruit
problem	above	wrinkly	responded	★grapefruit
finishes			tentacles	
screech				

★4. READING BY ANALOGY Have students figure out how to say /rō/ by reading other words they know.

no, mo, po, o, ★ro	po, polite	o, opened	ro, robot

5. ★NEW WORDS IN CONTEXT: OCTOPUS, SOFT, AND UNDERSIDE; MAIN IDEA AND SUPPORTING DETAILS See the Teacher's Guide.

The Octopus

An octopus is a strange-looking animal that lives under the sea. It has a big, soft body with no bones. An octopus has eight long tentacles that stretch from its body. Suckers cover the underside of these long arms. An octopus is at home in its deep sea habitat. However, if an octopus came to visit you, it would be an alien in your home.

6. DAILY STORY READING

51

WORKING TOWARD MASTERY

Repeat practice with each exercise to build mastery. Mix group and individual turns, independent of your voice.

◆◆ WORD CLUES

Add variety to the Exercise.

- Have students find a section.
  Find A2.
- Give a word clue.
  When something is wrong, you have this.
- Have students touch the word.
  Touch the word in A2 that tells what you have when something is wrong.
- Have students read the word.
  Read the word.
  (problem)
- Have students use the word in a sentence.

Sentence Suggestions: Use sentences *after* decoding the individual word. Using sentences emphasizes that words have meaning.

◆◆ Repeat and extend practice for English Language Learners and students with language delays.

★ 4 READING BY ANALOGY

- Have students practice the open syllable /ō/ words. Say something like:

  Read the first word. (no)

  The next syllables rhyme with "no." Read the syllables. (/mō/, /pō/, /ō/, /rō/)

  Now read the syllables and then the words. (/pō/-polite; /ō/-opened; /rō/-robot)

- Repeat practice. Mix group and individual turns, independent of your voice.

5 NEW WORDS IN CONTEXT, MAIN IDEA AND SUPPORTING DETAILS

★ New Words in Context: octopus, soft, underside

- Have students read the paragraph silently.
- Then have students read the paragraph out loud. Practice any difficult words and reread.

Main Idea and Supporting Details

- Draw a main idea graphic organizer on the chalkboard or a chart.
- Demonstrate and guide students as you complete a main idea graphic organizer.

  What does the main idea tell about? (The whole paragraph)

  Today, you're going to help me figure out the main idea.

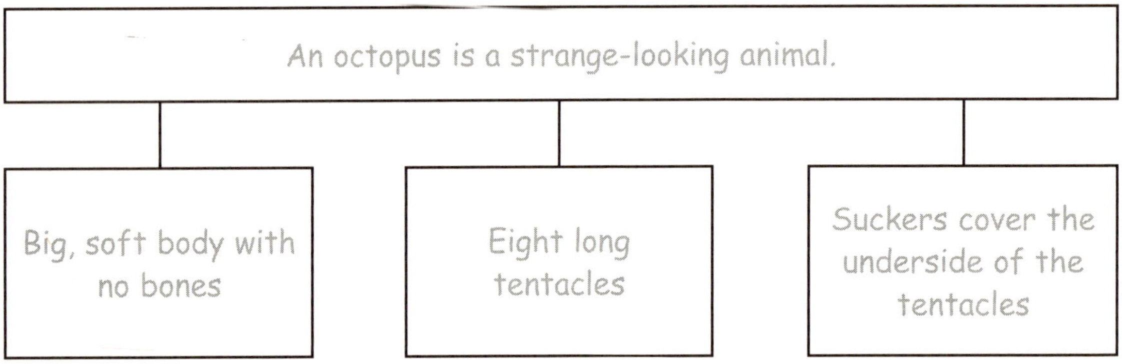

Have students identify the topic of the paragraph. Write the topic in the top box.

What is the topic of the paragraph? (An octopus)

Have students read the underlined detail. Then write the supporting detail in a box.

Look at your Exercise. What's the first detail about an octopus? (It has a big, soft body with no bones.) That detail explains why an octopus is strange looking.

- Help students identify the second and third detail. Write the details in the boxes.
- Help students construct and locate a main idea statement.

  Let's read all the details. What are all the details about? (An octopus)

  What do the details tell us about an octopus? An octopus is . . . a strange-looking animal.

  That's one way to say the main idea. Another way to say the main idea might be "An octopus would be an alien on land."

6 DAILY STORY READING—See Daily Lesson Planning.

7 COMPREHENSION AND SKILL ACTIVITIES—See Daily Lesson Planning.

Unit 47 Exercise 3
For use with Story 3

1. SOUND REVIEW Use the Sound Cards for Units 39–47 and selected Review Cards.

2. SOUND AND SENTENCE PRACTICE Have students read the sentence, then identify the words with underlined sounds. Next, read the underlined sounds.

> The alien's knobby knees knock when it walks.
> It also makes noise with its huge voice.
> Listen to its metal body groan, moan, and croak.

★3. ACCURACY/FLUENCY BUILDING For each section, have students read any underlined part, then read each word. Next, have students read the whole column and identify what's the same about each word. ADVANCED ACCURACY/FLUENCY Have students read the word first, then read the underlined sound.

A1 Sound Practice	**B1** Bossy E	**C1** Word Endings	**D1** Multisyllabic Words	**E1** Sound Review
since	sides	wrapped	teach-er	chewed
voice	beside	stretched	fat-ter	pointed
place	grape	gulped	sneak-er	louder
noticed	**B2** Sound Practice	stick	shut-tle	saw
change	bread	sticking	re-spond-ed	**E2** Tricky Words
page	read	crunch	ten-ta-cles	★shove
large	head	crunching	teacher	★shoved
A2 Sound Review	ahead	finish	fatter	★nudge
heel	across	finishes	sneaker	★nudged
ribs	away	wrinkle	shuttle	★fruit
problem	above	wrinkly	responded	★grapefruit
finishes			tentacles	
screech				

★4. READING BY ANALOGY Have students figure out how to say /rō/ by reading other words they know.

no, mo, po, o, ★ro	po, polite	o, opened	ro, robot

5. ★NEW WORDS IN CONTEXT: OCTOPUS, SOFT, AND UNDERSIDE; MAIN IDEA AND SUPPORTING DETAILS See the Teacher's Guide.

The Octopus

An octopus is a strange-looking animal that lives under the sea. It has a big, soft body with no bones. An octopus has eight long tentacles that stretch from its body. Suckers cover the underside of these long arms. An octopus is at home in its deep sea habitat. However, if an octopus came to visit you, it would be an alien in your home.

6. DAILY STORY READING

51

PROCEDURES

1. Introduction

Have students summarize Chapters 1–2 by following the gray text in the storybook.

2. First Reading

- Mix group and individual turns, independent of your voice. Have students work toward an accuracy goal of 0–2 errors. Gently correct and quietly keep track of errors made by all students in the group.
- After reading the story, practice any difficult words.

3. Optional Second Reading

If the group has not reached the accuracy goal or is reading dysfluently, have the group reread the story, mixing group and individual turns.

4. Repeated Readings

a. Short Passage Practice

Select short passages from the story. Demonstrate expressive, fluent reading. Guide practice with your voice. Then provide individual turns.

b. Partner Reading

During students' daily independent work, have them do Partner Reading.

5. Homework 3

Have students read the story at home. (*Read Well Plus* Homework is available in blackline masters.)

STORY 3

CHAPTER 3
A Sneaker Snack

Who are the main characters?[1] What is Asha's problem?[2] Why doesn't Asha want her teacher to know about the problem?[3] What is unusual about the children's teacher?[4]

"Why did you bring the problem to school if the teacher will take it away?" Maria asked.

Asha responded, "Where would I keep it? The aliens chew through everything. I put it in my backpack, so it wouldn't be a problem."

Maria wasn't sure that was very smart. Asha's air tank was in her backpack. If the problem chewed up the tank, Asha wouldn't have any air if she needed it.

"I gave it my shoe to eat," Asha said.

"Your sneaker?" Maria asked. "What if the alien doesn't like to eat shoes?"

Asha said, "It was eating them when I found it, so . . ." Asha shrugged.

Show me what Asha did. What does it mean when someone shrugs?[5]

12

1. **Summarizing, Identifying—Who (Main Characters)** (Asha and Maria are the main characters.)
2. **Summarizing, Identifying—Problem** (Asha's problem is that she has a small alien that she calls "a problem" in her backpack. The aliens eat everything, and it might eat Asha's air tank.)
3. **Inferring, Explaining** (Asha doesn't want her teacher to know about the problem because it would take the problem away from her.)
4. **Inferring** (The children's teacher is a robot.)
5. **Demonstrating, Defining Vocabulary—Shrugs**

Just then, the robot teacher said, "It is time to go." One by one the kids went into the shuttle. Maria and Asha sat in the back so they could open Asha's backpack and look at the problem.

The problem was a wrinkly ball about the size of a grapefruit, with tentacles sticking out on all sides and a mouth almost as wide as its body. The shoe beside it was missing most of the heel. While the girls watched, the problem pulled part of the sneaker into its mouth. There was a crunching sound, and the problem grew a little fatter.

Close your eyes and imagine what the alien would look like. Describe the alien.[1] Now look at the picture on the next page. Why are the aliens a problem for the space station?[2] Why is it a problem for Asha to have the problem in her backpack?[3] In the next chapter, you'll find that the problem gets bigger![4]

1. **Visualizing, Describing, Using Vocabulary—Alien** (The alien was about the size of a grapefruit with tentacles sticking out on all sides. It had a mouth almost as big as its body, and it looked like a wrinkly ball.)
2. **Inferring—Problem** (The aliens were eating and chewing through everything.)
3. **Inferring, Explaining** (The problem was eating all of Asha's things. It might eat her air tank.)
4. **Previewing**

MAIN IDEA AND SUPPORTING DETAILS

CHECKOUT OPPORTUNITY

Listen to your students read individually while others work.

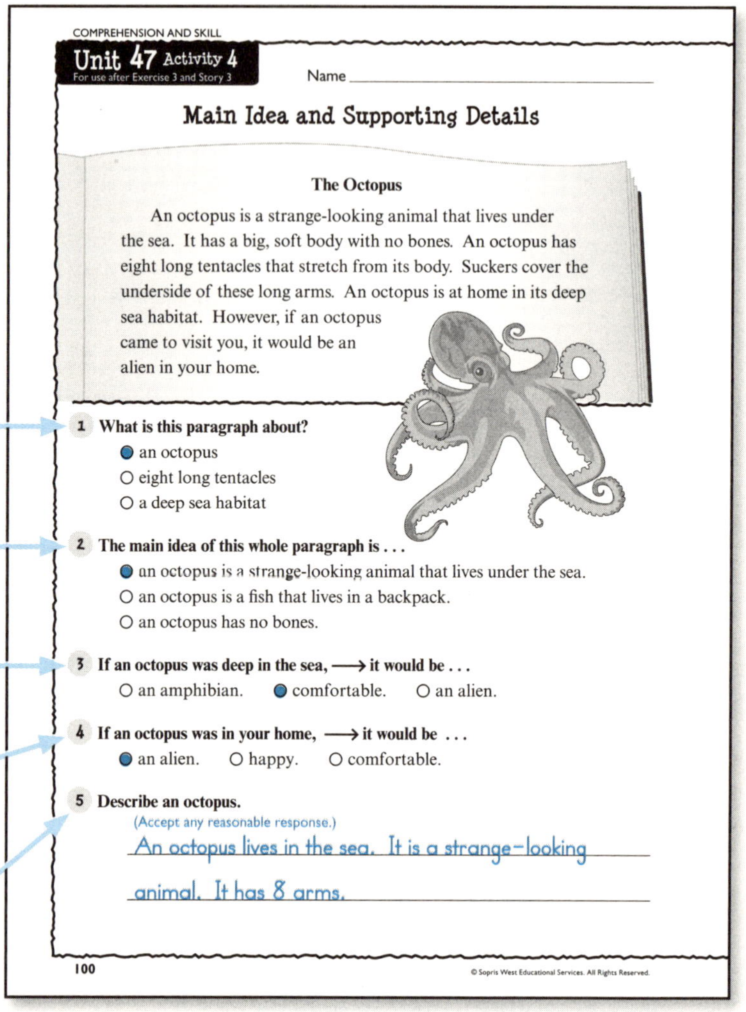

COMPREHENSION AND SKILL

Unit 47 Activity 4

For use after Exercise 3 and Story 3

Name ______________________

Main Idea and Supporting Details

The Octopus

An octopus is a strange-looking animal that lives under the sea. It has a big, soft body with no bones. An octopus has eight long tentacles that stretch from its body. Suckers cover the underside of these long arms. An octopus is at home in its deep sea habitat. However, if an octopus came to visit you, it would be an alien in your home.

1 **What is this paragraph about?**
- ● an octopus
- ○ eight long tentacles
- ○ a deep sea habitat

2 **The main idea of this whole paragraph is . . .**
- ● an octopus is a strange-looking animal that lives under the sea.
- ○ an octopus is a fish that lives in a backpack.
- ○ an octopus has no bones.

3 **If an octopus was deep in the sea, ⟶ it would be . . .**
○ an amphibian. ● comfortable. ○ an alien.

4 **If an octopus was in your home, ⟶ it would be . . .**
● an alien. ○ happy. ○ comfortable.

5 **Describe an octopus.**
(Accept any reasonable response.)
An octopus lives in the sea. It is a strange-looking animal. It has 8 arms.

100

© Sopris West Educational Services. All Rights Reserved.

Identifying—Topic

Identifying—Main Idea

Identifying—Cause and Effect

Identifying—Cause and Effect
Using Vocabulary—Alien

Describing
Complete Sentence,
Conventions—Beginning Capital, Period

PROCEDURES

For each step, demonstrate and guide practice as needed.

Paragraph Comprehension—Basic Instructions

- Have students read the paragraph to themselves.
- Have students mark the correct answers, write answers in the blanks, and use capital letters and periods where appropriate.

Note: Neat work helps students take pride in their efforts. Periodically, comment on students' progress and best efforts.

SENTENCE JUMBLE

Sequencing
Complete Sentence,
Conventions—Beginning Capital, Period

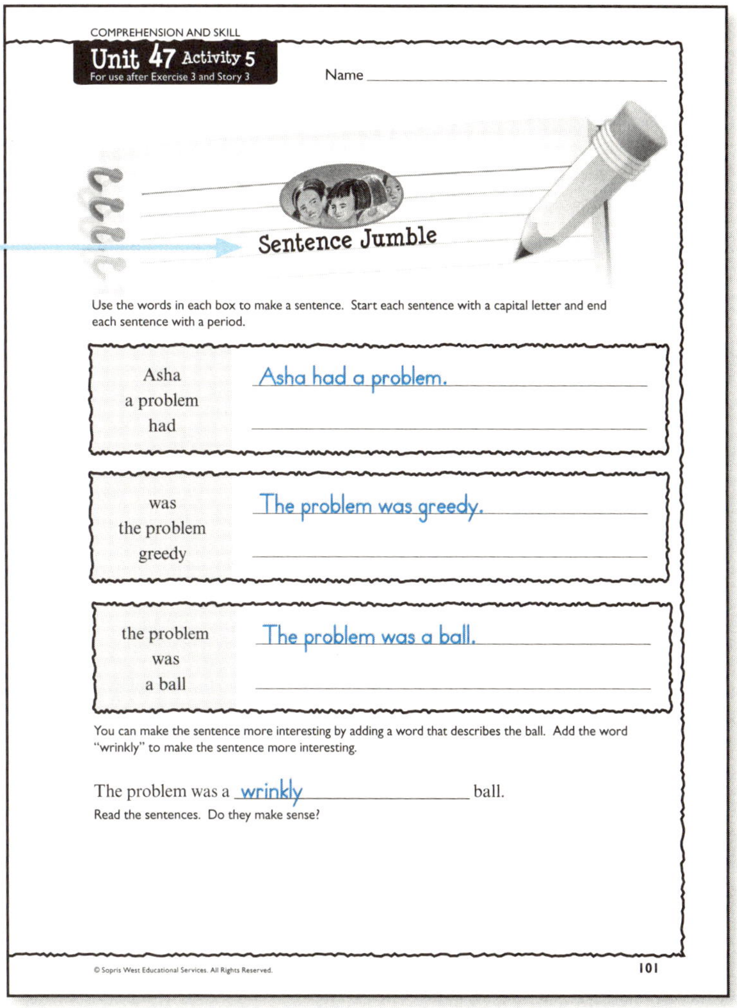
COMPREHENSION AND SKILL
Unit 47 Activity 5
For use after Exercise 3 and Story 3

Name ______________________

Sentence Jumble

Use the words in each box to make a sentence. Start each sentence with a capital letter and end each sentence with a period.

Asha a problem had	Asha had a problem.
was the problem greedy	The problem was greedy.
the problem was a ball	The problem was a ball.

You can make the sentence more interesting by adding a word that describes the ball. Add the word "wrinkly" to make the sentence more interesting.

The problem was a wrinkly ball.

Read the sentences. Do they make sense?

© Sopris West Educational Services. All Rights Reserved. 101

CHECKOUT OPPORTUNITY

Listen to your students read individually while others work.

PROCEDURES

For each step, demonstrate and guide practice as needed.

1. Sequencing Words—Specific Instructions (Boxes 1–3)

- Have students read the words in the first box.

  Have students identify who or what the sentence will be about and determine the word sequence.

  Who is the sentence about? (Asha) So your sentence will start with "Asha."

  Does "Asha a problem had" make sense? (No)

  Does "Asha had a problem" make sense? (Yes)

  Have students write the sentence starting with a capital and ending with a period.

  So you will write "Asha had a problem." Start with a capital and end with a period.

- Repeat with the second and third boxes.

2. Sentence Completion—Specific Instructions (Last item)

Have students write the descriptive word "wrinkly" to complete the sentence.

❶ SOUND REVIEW

Use the Sound Cards from Units 39–47 and selected Review Sound Cards and Tricky Word Cards.

❷ SOUND AND SENTENCE PRACTICE

❸ ACCURACY AND FLUENCY BUILDING

Provide repeated practice, building accuracy first, then fluency.

Note: For advanced practice, have students read the word, then any underlined part.

B3. Reading by Analogy

- Have students read each underlined syllable and the word.
  All of the first syllables in the next words rhyme with "no."
  Read each underlined syllable and then the word.
  (/mō/-moment, /pō/-polite, /ō/-open, /rō/-robot)
  These words are all alike because they all begin with syllables that rhyme with "no."
- Repeat practice, mixing group and individual turns.

C2 and D1. Multisyllabic Words

- For the list of words divided by syllables, have students read each syllable out loud and finger count how many syllables are in the word.
  Use each word in a sentence as appropriate.

beside	2 syllables	He wasn't behind me, he was . . . *beside* me.
fatter	2 syllables	The [bear] ate so much it grew even . . . (*fatter*).
sneakers	2 syllables	She tied the laces on her . . . (*sneakers*).
problem	2 syllables	Our teacher had us solve a difficult math . . . (*problem*).
station	2 syllables	We packed our bags and went to the train . . . *station*.
pointed	2 syllables	The end of that pencil is very . . . *pointed*.
finishes	3 syllables	The race is so hard, I hope she . . . *finishes*.
responded	3 syllables	He asked a question and she answered. She . . . *responded* to the question.
tentacles	3 syllables	An octopus has eight long arms called . . . (*tentacles*).

- For the list of whole words, build accuracy and then fluency. Repeat, mixing group and individual turns.

❹ TRICKY WORDS IN CONTEXT

❺ AFFIX PRACTICE

- Have students identify the affix /-tion/.
- For each word, have students read the underlined affix, then the whole word.
- Repeat practice. Mix group and individual turns, independent of your voice.

❻ DAILY STORY READING—See Daily Lesson Planning.

❼ COMPREHENSION AND SKILL ACTIVITIES—See Daily Lesson Planning.

Unit 47 Exercise 4

For use with Story 4 as needed

1. SOUND REVIEW Use the Sound Cards for Units 39–47 and selected Review Cards.

2. SOUND AND SENTENCE PRACTICE Have students read the sentence, then identify the words with underlined sounds. Next, read the underlined sounds.

> Listen to the alien's metal body groan, moan, and croak.
> The alien makes noise with its screechy voice.
> Its knobby knees knock when it walks.

3. ACCURACY/FLUENCY BUILDING For each section, have students read any underlined part, then read each word. Next, have students read the whole column and identify what's the same about each word. ADVANCED ACCURACY/FLUENCY Have students read the word first, then read the underlined sound.

A1 Sound Practice
- large
- charge
- change
- place
- voice
- noticed

A2 Sound Review
- gulped
- wrapped
- stretched
- sticking
- crunching

B1 Sound Practice
- oil
- coin
- join

B2 Rhyming Words
- head
- read
- bread

B3 Reading by Analogy
- no
- moment
- polite
- open
- robot

C1 Sound Practice
- write
- wrote
- wrap
- wrinkle
- wrinkly

C2 Multisyllabic Words
- be-side
- fat-ter
- sneak-ers
- beside
- fatter
- sneakers

D1 Multisyllabic Words
- prob-lem
- sta-tion
- point-ed
- fin-ish-es
- re-spond-ed
- ten-ta-cles
- problem
- station
- pointed
- finishes
- responded
- tentacles

E1 Sound Review
- grew
- saw
- grow
- chew
- draw
- grown
- road
- boat
- coast

E2 Tricky Words
- fruit
- grapefruit

4. TRICKY WORDS IN CONTEXT See the Teacher's Guide.

Maria wanted Asha to look in her backpack, so she nudged her in the ribs.	nudged
He took the whole thing and shoved it in his mouth.	shoved

5. AFFIX PRACTICE Have students read the underlined part then the whole word.

fiction	station	nation	vacation

6. DAILY STORY READING

52

WHAT TO DO IF . . .
(Reminder)

If a student misidentifies a sound when reading a word, write the word on a chalkboard.

- Have everyone identify the correct sound.
- Have students sound out the word or syllable.
- Have students read the word.
- Proceed with the lesson, but return to the word at least three times.
- Acknowledge students' efforts when they correctly identify the difficult word. You read the hard word . . . once, twice, three times!

◆◆ SENTENCE SUGGESTIONS

(B1) join—[Joey] wants to . . . *join* the [team].

(B2) read—That was a book she had never . . . *read*.

(C1) write—I am going to . . . *write* [a story].

(C1) wrote—Yesterday, I . . . *wrote* [two stories].

(E1) grew—Last year, I . . . *grew* [carrots in my garden].

(E1) grow—This year, I will . . . *grow* [tomatoes in my garden].

Sentence Suggestions: Use sentences *after* decoding the individual word. Using sentences emphasizes that words have meaning.

◆◆ Repeat and extend practice for English Language Learners and students with language delays.

PROCEDURES

1. Introduction

Have students summarize Chapters 1–3 by explaining who the story was about and something about the problem.

2. First and Second Reading

- Have students whisper read Chapter 4.
- Have students read Chapter 4 out loud.
  Mix group and individual turns.
  Have students word toward an accuracy goal of 0–2 errors.
  Quietly keep track of errors made by all students in the group.
  Gently correct any errors and have students reread the sentence.
- After reading the story, practice any difficult words.

3. Repeated Readings

a. Timed Readings

As time allows, have students do Timed Readings while others follow along.

b. Partner Reading

During students' daily independent work, have them do Partner Reading.

4. Homework 4

Have students read the story at home. (*Read Well Plus* Homework is available in blackline masters.)

CHAPTER 4

A Bigger Problem

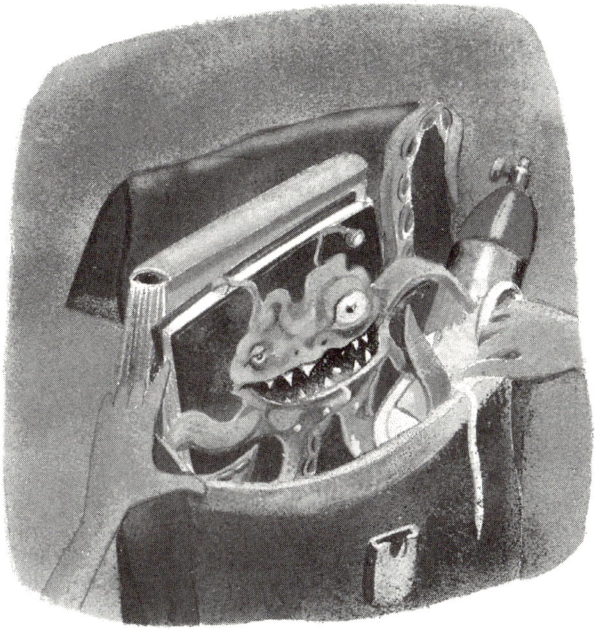

The problem in Asha's backpack was having a wonderful meal of Asha's sneaker. "What are you going to do when it finishes your shoes?" Maria asked.

"I hadn't thought about that," Asha said.

Look at the problem. Do you think it will cause any problems on the field trip?[1]

1 Inferring, Predicting, Teacher Think Aloud
Some of you think the problem in Asha's backpack could cause problems on the field trip. The problem seems harmless. What do you think it might do?

STORY 4

The shuttle left the station, and the teacher started talking about the asteroid mine they were going to see. Asha and Maria tried to listen, but Maria heard a metal screech from Asha's pack. Maria looked into the backpack. The problem had grown! The shoes were gone, and it was working on the air tank.

Maria nudged Asha in the ribs and pointed into her pack. Asha's eyes grew wide. She grabbed for the tank, but the problem wrapped its tentacles around the tank and shoved it into its mouth. In one loud gulp, the air tank was gone!

"What do we do now?" Asha asked.

"I don't know," said Maria. "The problem is bigger, but it's still all wrinkly. I don't think it's full yet!"

"I noticed that too," gulped Asha. Then her voice got louder. "What are we going to do?"

This sounds dangerous. What do you think the girls should do?[1]

15

1 Making Connections, Inferring

AFFIRMING PREDICTIONS

After reading, have students discuss whether their earlier predictions about the problem were correct.

STORY 4

"What do we do about what?" the teacher asked. It stretched its neck out across the length of the shuttle until its head was right in front of the two girls. Then it saw what was in Asha's pack.

What do you think will happen next?

16

1 Predicting

VISUALIZING AND ILLUSTRATING

Visualizing, Illustrating—Who (Characters), Setting, Action

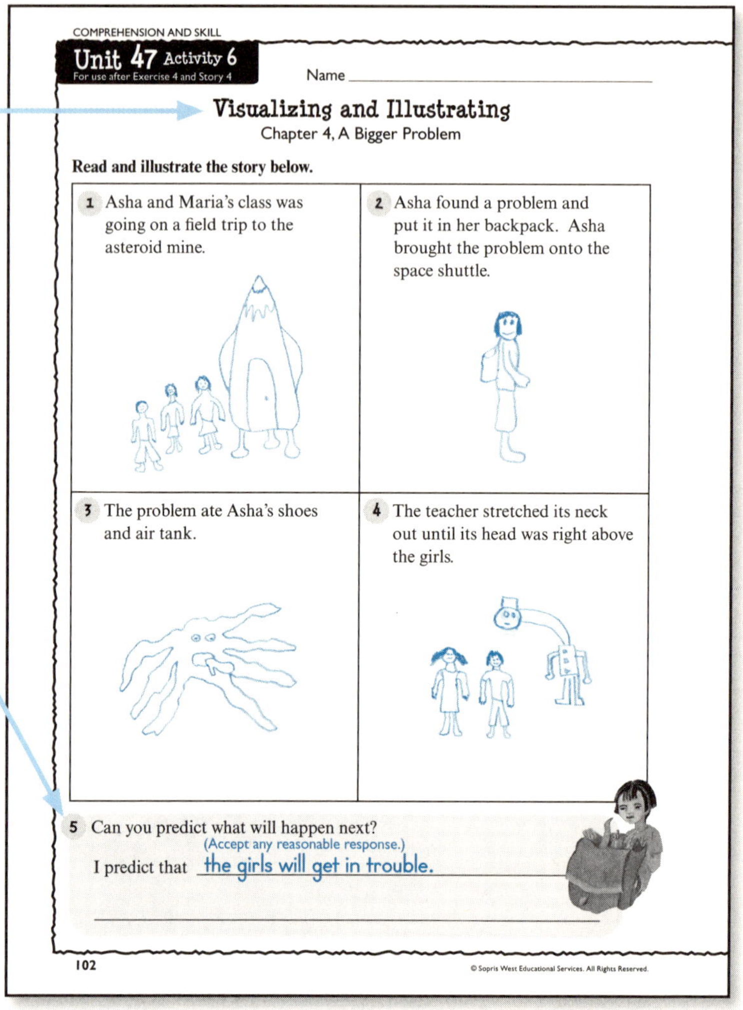

COMPREHENSION AND SKILL

Unit 47 Activity 6
For use after Exercise 4 and Story 4

Name ____________________

Visualizing and Illustrating
Chapter 4, A Bigger Problem

Read and illustrate the story below.

1 Asha and Maria's class was going on a field trip to the asteroid mine.

2 Asha found a problem and put it in her backpack. Asha brought the problem onto the space shuttle.

3 The problem ate Asha's shoes and air tank.

4 The teacher stretched its neck out until its head was right above the girls.

5 Can you predict what will happen next?
(Accept any reasonable response.)
I predict that the girls will get in trouble.

102

© Sopris West Educational Services. All Rights Reserved.

Predicting
Conventions—Period

CHECKOUT OPPORTUNITY
Listen to your students read individually while others work.

PROCEDURES

For each step, demonstrate and guide practice as needed.

1. Visualization and Illustration—Basic Instructions (Items 1–4)

- For each item, have students read the item, then close their eyes and imagine a picture.
- Have students illustrate each item.

Note: Help children be at ease with illustrating. Demonstrate how to make a simple drawing. Model a sense of humor.

2. Sentence Completion—Basic Instructions (Item 5)

- Have students read the question and brainstorm possible responses.
- Have students complete the sentence and end it with a period.

ALPHABETICAL ORDER AND MY PICTURE DICTIONARY

Alphabetical Order

Defining Vocabulary—Alien
Visualizing, Illustrating

Defining, Using Vocabulary—Habitat
Complete Sentence,
Conventions—Beginning Capital, Period
Visualizing, Illustrating

Defining, Using Vocabulary—Robot
Complete Sentence,
Conventions—Beginning Capital, Period
Visualizing, Illustrating

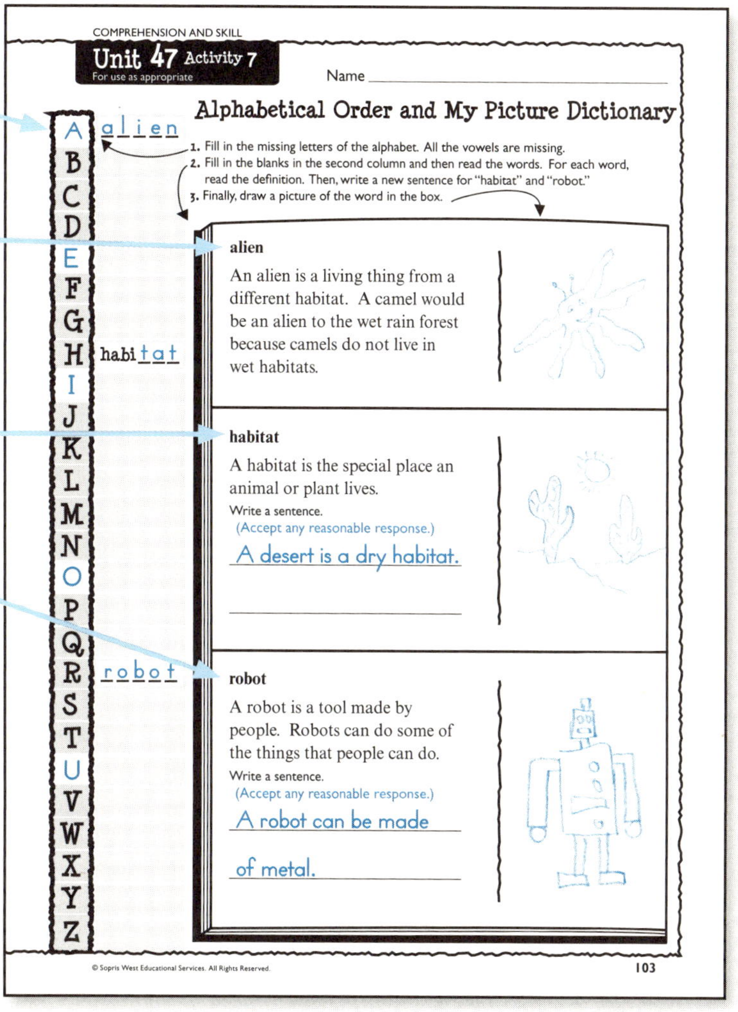

COMPREHENSION AND SKILL
Unit 47 Activity 7
For use as appropriate

Name ____________

Alphabetical Order and My Picture Dictionary

1. Fill in the missing letters of the alphabet. All the vowels are missing.
2. Fill in the blanks in the second column and then read the words. For each word, read the definition. Then, write a new sentence for "habitat" and "robot."
3. Finally, draw a picture of the word in the box.

A B C D E F G H I J K L M N O P Q R S T U V W X Y Z

alien

habitat

robot

alien

An alien is a living thing from a different habitat. A camel would be an alien to the wet rain forest because camels do not live in wet habitats.

habitat

A habitat is the special place an animal or plant lives.

Write a sentence.
(Accept any reasonable response.)
A desert is a dry habitat.

robot

A robot is a tool made by people. Robots can do some of the things that people can do.

Write a sentence.
(Accept any reasonable response.)
A robot can be made of metal.

© Sopris West Educational Services. All Rights Reserved.

103

CHECKOUT OPPORTUNITY

Listen to your students read individually while others work.

PROCEDURES

For each step, demonstrate and guide practice as needed.

1. Alphabetical Order—Basic Instructions

- Have students read and point to the letters. Tell students that the letters that are missing are called vowels. Have students fill in each missing letter.
- Repeat until the alphabet is complete.
- Have students fill in or complete the words and then read them. Tell them the words are in alphabetical order.

Note: Have students look at the defined words in the picture dictionary for clues on how to fill in the blanks.

2. My Picture Dictionary—Specific Instructions

- For the word "alien," have students read the word and the definition.
  Have students visualize an alien. Think aloud. Demonstrate illustrating an alien.
- For the word "habitat," have students brainstorm possible sentences that use the word.
  Demonstrate writing a sentence to extend the definition.
  Have students visualize a habitat. Think aloud. Demonstrate illustrating a habitat.
- Repeat the previous direction with "robot."

❶ SOUND REVIEW

Use the Sound Cards for Units 39–47 and selected Review Sound Cards and Tricky Word Cards.

❷ SOUND AND SENTENCE PRACTICE

- Have students read each sentence, then identify the underlined sounds.
- Repeat sentences to build accuracy and fluency.

❸ ACCURACY AND FLUENCY BUILDING

For each task, provide repeated practice, building accuracy first, then fluency.

C1. Compound Words

- Remind students that compound words are made up of two or more smaller words.

  Look at the first word. Read the first small word. (space)
  Read the next small word. (craft)
  Read the whole word. (spacecraft)

- Repeat practice. Mix group and individual turns, independent of your voice.

D1. Multisyllabic Words

- For the list of words divided by syllables, have students read each syllable out loud and finger count how many syllables are in the word.
  Use each word in a sentence as appropriate.

announced	2 syllables	At the relay race, our principal . . . *announced* the winners.
rescue	2 syllables	The dog was a specially trained search and . . . *rescue* dog.
arrive	2 syllables	We couldn't wait for our grandparents to . . . *arrive*.
couple	2 syllables	Another way to say "I have two [hats]" is "I have a . . . *couple* of [hats]."
shuttle's	2 syllables	While in space, they stored food in the space . . . *shuttle's* hold.

- For the list of whole words, build accuracy and then fluency. Repeat, mixing group and individual turns.

Note: New multisyllabic words that are slightly tricky are starred. Slashes through the silent letters provide support to students as they use the sounds they know to read the words.

(continued)

Unit 47 Exercise 5
For use with Story 5

1. SOUND REVIEW Use the Sound Cards for Units 39–47 and selected Review Cards.

2. SOUND AND SENTENCE PRACTICE Have students read the sentence, then identify the words with underlined sounds. Next, read the underlined sounds.

> The alien's voice makes screechy noises when it eats.
> The alien eats toast, roast, coins, soil, oil, and foil.

★3. ACCURACY/FLUENCY BUILDING For each section, have students read any underlined part, then read each word. Next, have students read the whole column and identify what's the same about each word. ADVANCED ACCURACY/FLUENCY Have students read the word first, then read the underlined sound.

A1	B1	C1	D1	E1
Sound Practice charge change danger call calm calmly **A2** **Sound Review** handle shreds split spun sense	**Bossy E** die inflate inflated explode exploded explosion **B2** **Sound Practice** circles notice chance since	**Compound Words** spacecraft lifeboat anyway anymore airlock's **C2** **Sound Practice** blown window follow floated groaned moaned	**Multisyllabic Words** ★an-nounced res-cue ★ar-rive ★cou-ple shut-tle's announced rescue arrive couple shuttle's	**Word Endings** peered pushed zipped puffed whooshed zoomed **E2** **Tricky Words** ★wherever ★against ★nervous ★they'd

★4. READING BY ANALOGY Have students figure out how to read words with the long /ī/ sound by reading words they know.

> bi, bicycle ★si, silence ★pi, pilot

5. MULTISYLLABIC CHALLENGE WORDS Have students say each word part, then read the word and its definition aloud.

> in-flate = inflate
> The boy will blow into the beach ball and inflate it.

> in-flat-ed = inflated
> The beach ball was filled with air. It was inflated.

> in-flat-a-ble = inflatable
> That beach ball can be filled with air. It is inflatable.

6. DAILY STORY READING

53

◆◆ SENTENCE SUGGESTIONS

(A1) call—She wanted to talk to her friend, so she decided to . . . *call.*

(A2) sense—We couldn't understand how the alien could eat so much. It didn't make . . . *sense.*

(B1) die—We didn't want the alien to . . . *die.*

(C1) anymore—He got up because he didn't want to sleep . . . *anymore.*

(C2) blown—The wind was so strong, my window was . . . *blown* open.

Sentence Suggestions: Use sentences *after* decoding the individual word. Using sentences emphasizes that words have meaning.

◆◆ Repeat and extend practice for English Language Learners and students with language delays.

E2. Tricky Words

★ **New Tricky Words: wherever, against, nervous, they'd**

- For each new Tricky Word, have students identify known parts of the word. Use the word in a sentence, or tell students the word as appropriate.

  wherever
  Look at the first word. It's just a little tricky. You know the first part of the word.
  Tell me the word. (where) Now read the whole word. (wherever)
  I said I didn't care where we went, and I would go . . . *wherever.*
  What kind of word is "wherever"? (A compound word)
  What are the two smaller words? (where and ever)

  against The bookshelf fell over when he leaned . . . *against* it.
  nervous Her legs were shaking because she was . . . *nervous.*
  they'd A short way to say "they would" is . . . *they'd.*

- Have students read the words, building accuracy, then fluency. Repeat, mixing group and individual turns, independent of your voice.

★ 4 READING BY ANALOGY

- Have students practice the open syllable /ī/ words. Say something like:
  Read the word part and the word. (/bī/-bicycle)
  The next syllable rhymes with /bī/. Read the word part and the word. (/sī/-silence)
  The next syllable rhymes with /bī/ and /sī/. Read the word part and the word. (/pī/-pilot)
- Repeat practice. Mix group and individual turns, independent of your voice.

5 MULTISYLLABIC CHALLENGE WORDS

- Tell students that they can read almost any word by using the sounds and parts of words they already know. Say something like: Look at the first word. What does i-n say? (in)
  What's on the end of the word? (A Bossy E)
  So, what does the next syllable say? (flate)
  Read the whole word. (inflate)
  Now read the sentence. (The boy will blow into the beach ball and *inflate* it.)
  Watch me inflate the beach ball. What am I doing to the beach ball? (Inflating it)
- For each remaining word, guide students through the process of identifying the unknown words, using the sounds and parts of words they know.

6 DAILY STORY READING—See Daily Lesson Planning.

7 COMPREHENSION AND SKILL ACTIVITIES—See Daily Lesson Planning.

Unit 47 Exercise 5
For use with Story 5

1. SOUND REVIEW Use the Sound Cards for Units 39–47 and selected Review Cards.

2. SOUND AND SENTENCE PRACTICE Have students read the sentence, then identify the words with underlined sounds. Next, read the underlined sounds.

The alien's voice makes screechy noises when it eats.
The alien eats toast, roast, coins, soil, oil, and foil.

★3. ACCURACY/FLUENCY BUILDING For each section, have students read any underlined part, then read each word. Next, have students read the whole column and identify what's the same about each word. ADVANCED ACCURACY/FLUENCY Have students read the word first, then read the underlined sound.

A1 Sound Practice	B1 Bossy E	C1 Compound Words	D1 Multisyllabic Words	E1 Word Endings
charge	die	spacecraft	★an-nounced	peered
change	inflate	lifeboat	res-cue	pushed
danger	inflated	anyway	★ar-rive	zipped
call	explode	anymore	★cou-ple	puffed
calm	exploded	airlock's	shut-tle's	whooshed
calmly	explosion	**C2** Sound Practice	announced	zoomed
A2 Sound Review	**B2** Sound Practice	blown	rescue	**E2** Tricky Words
handle	circles	window	arrive	★wherever
shreds	notice	follow	couple	★against
split	chance	floated	shuttle's	★nervous
spun	since	groaned		★they'd
sense		moaned		

★4. READING BY ANALOGY Have students figure out how to read words with the long /ī/ sound by reading words they know.

bi, bicycle ★si, silence ★pi, pilot

5. MULTISYLLABIC CHALLENGE WORDS Have students say each word part, then read the word and its definition aloud.

in-flate = inflate
The boy will blow into the beach ball and inflate it.

in-flat-ed = inflated
The beach ball was filled with air. It was inflated.

in-flat-a-ble = inflatable
That beach ball can be filled with air. It is inflatable.

6. DAILY STORY READING

53

WORKING WITH MULTIPLE GROUPS (Reminder)

If students are working independently, periodically scan the room while you teach. Provide appropriate, positive, descriptive feedback.

PROCEDURES

1. Introduction

Have students summarize what is known about the problem by following the gray text.

2. First Reading

- Mix group and individual turns, independent of your voice. Have students work toward an accuracy goal of 0–2 errors. Quietly keep track of errors made by all students in the group. Gently correct any error and have students reread the sentence.
- After reading the story, practice any difficult words.

3. Optional Second Reading

If the group has not reached the accuracy goal or is reading dysfluently, have the group reread the story, mixing group and individual turns.

4. Repeated Readings

a. Short Passage Practice

Select short passages from the story. Demonstrate expressive, fluent reading. Guide practice with your voice. Then provide individual turns.

b. Partner Reading

During students' daily independent work, have them do Partner Reading.

5. Homework 5

Have students read the story at home. (*Read Well Plus* Homework is available in blackline masters.)

STORY 5

CHAPTER 5

The Rescue Ball

Describe the problem.[1] Explain how it has grown.[2]

The girls were getting nervous. The problem was getting bigger, and the teacher had seen it. The teacher saw what was in Asha's pack and said, "You have a problem!"

Asha was too frightened to hide the problem. "It just ate my air tank!"

"Then I'm afraid we all have a problem," the teacher said. "It is just a matter of time before there is an explosion." Then the teacher calmly said, "Put your pack into the airlock."

"But the problem will die!" Asha cried.

The robot teacher said, "When the air tank explodes, the problem will die anyway." Then the robot teacher added, "And so will we."

How do you think Asha and Maria feel?[3] Who needs a rescue?[4]

17

1. **Describing** (The problem looks like a wrinkly ball, about the size of a grapefruit, with tentacles. Its mouth is almost as wide as its body.)
2. **Explaining, Inferring** (The problem has grown bigger every time it has eaten something. It ate Asha's shoes and her air tank.)
3. **Inferring, Making Connections** (Afraid, worried . . .)
4. **Inferring, Using Vocabulary—Rescue** (Asha and Maria need a rescue. The problem needs a rescue.)

Maria said, "We could put the problem in a rescue ball. Then maybe it would have a chance in space."

The teacher said, "That makes sense." It pulled a rescue ball off the wall and zipped it open. "Put your backpack in here," it said.

"What about my books and my music?" Asha asked.

Maria peered inside the backpack. "It ate those too," Maria said.

Asha pushed her backpack into the rescue ball. The teacher pulled a cord on the ball and it inflated with air. Then the teacher threw the ball into the airlock, closed the door, and pulled the handle. The airlock's outside door opened with a whoosh, and the rescue ball was blown out into space.

How did the teacher solve the problem? 1 The problem is floating out in space inside the rescue ball. If you were on the space shuttle with the children, what would you do next? 2 Read Chapter 6 to find out what happens to the problem. 3

❶ **Inferring, Explaining** (The teacher had Asha put her backpack in a rescue ball. Then the teacher released the problem into space.)

❷ **Applying, Explaining** (I would look out the window to see what happened next.)

❸ **Reading for Purpose**

FOCUS ON FLUENCY
(Reminder)

Short Passage Practice is an effective procedure for developing fluency. After completing a story, provide Short Passage Practice on a regular basis with students who are reading less than 109 words correct per minute on assessments.

With each paragraph or short passage, demonstrate expressive, fluent reading. Guide practice with your voice. Then provide individual turns.

MAIN IDEA AND SUPPORTING DETAILS

CHECKOUT OPPORTUNITY

Listen to your students read individually while others work.

Identifying—Topic

Identifying—Main Idea, Facts (Supporting Details)
Conventions—Beginning Capital

COMPREHENSION AND SKILL
Unit 47 Activity 8
For use after Exercise 5 and Story 5

Name ____________________

Main Idea and Supporting Details

Jellyfish

Jellyfish are interesting animals that live in the sea. Jellyfish have no bones, clear bodies, and no brains. Jellyfish have hundreds of tentacles that sting and catch food. Jellyfish are at home in their deep sea habitat. However, if a jellyfish were put on the moon, it would be an alien.

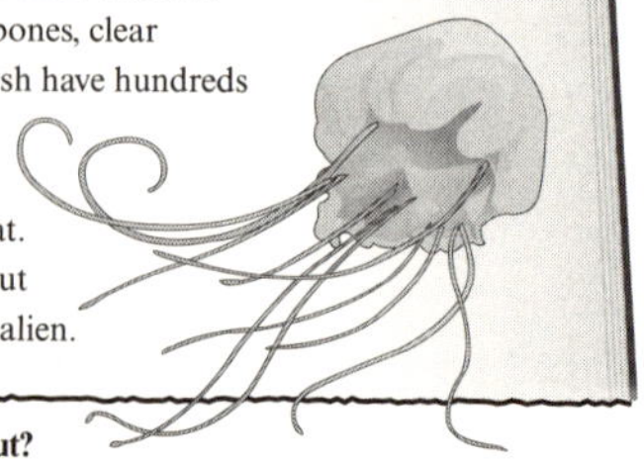

1 **What is the whole paragraph about?**

○ tentacles ○ brains ● jellyfish

2 **Write "Jellyfish" on the line below. The sentence tells the main idea of the passage. Next, write three facts that tell about the main idea. There are more than three facts. Pick your favorites.**

Main Idea

Jellyfish __________ are interesting animals that live in the sea.

(Accept any reasonable response.)

Fact 1	Fact 2	Fact 3
No bones	No brains	Hundreds of tentacles that sting

104

PROCEDURES

For each step, demonstrate and guide practice as needed.

Paragraph Comprehension—Basic Instructions

- Have students read the paragraph to themselves.
- Have students mark the correct answers, write answers in the blanks, and use beginning capitals when appropriate.

Note: If time permits, you may wish to have students list the supporting details using complete sentences.

★ STORY COMPLETION

CHECKOUT OPPORTUNITY

Listen to your students read individually while others work.

Complete Sentence, Conventions—Beginning Capital, Period

Describing

Identifying—Action

Complete Sentence, Conventions—Beginning Capital, Period

Visualizing, Illustrating

COMPREHENSION AND SKILL

Unit 47 Activity 9

For use as appropriate

Name ____________

★ Story Completion

Our class went on a field trip to the moon. There was no air on the moon, so we carried air tanks on our backs. It was a great trip. We could see Earth floating in space below us. Then, we saw a fantastic sight.

1 Use the words in the box to make a sentence.

an alien
us
greeted

An alien greeted us.

2 Make the sentence more interesting by adding the word "bicolored" to describe the alien.

A bicolored alien greeted us.

3 Choose what happens next.

(Accept any reasonable response.)

The alien . . .

● smiled and shook our hands.

○ screeched and ran away.

4 Write a sentence to end the story.

Soon the alien was our friend.

Read the story. Does it make sense? Draw a picture of the bicolored alien in the box above.

105

PROCEDURES

For each step, demonstrate and guide practice as needed.

1. Sequencing Words—Basic Instructions (Item 1)

- Have students read the paragraph.
- Have students read the words in the box, identify who or what the sentence will be about, and determine the word sequence.
- Have students write the sentence starting with a capital and ending with a period.

2. Sentence Completion—Specific Instructions (Item 2)

Have students write the descriptive word "bicolored" to complete the sentence.

3. Multiple Choice—Basic Instructions (Item 3)

Have students fill in the bubble of their choice.

4. Sentence Writing—Basic Instructions (Item 4)

- Have students read the direction and brainstorm possible responses.
- Have students write a sentence, starting with a capital and ending with a period.
- Have students complete an illustration of a bicolored alien.

❶ SOUND REVIEW

❷ SOUND AND SENTENCE PRACTICE

❸ ACCURACY AND FLUENCY BUILDING

Provide repeated practice, building accuracy first, then fluency.

Note: For advanced practice, have students read the word, then any underlined part.

C1. Multisyllabic Words

- Have students read each syllable out loud and finger count how many syllables are in the word.

  Use the word in a sentence as appropriate.

station	2 syllables	Astronauts can spend months on a space . . . *station.*
appeared	2 syllables	I couldn't find my book, and suddenly it . . . *appeared.*
allowed	2 syllables	My teacher said running in the halls was not . . . *allowed.*
asteroids	3 syllables	Big chunks of rock that orbit the Sun are . . . *asteroids.*
excitement	3 syllables	I was so happy, I couldn't contain my . . . *excitement.*
tentacles	3 syllables	Do you think aliens have long arms called . . . *tentacles?*
responded	3 syllables	The teacher asked questions. The class . . . *responded.*

- Repeat the list, building accuracy and then fluency. Mix group and individual turns, independent of your voice.

❹ NEW WORDS IN CONTEXT, FLUENCY PASSAGE

★ **New Tricky Words: brains, jellyfish, sting**

Fluency Passage

- Demonstrate how to pause briefly at commas in a series.

  Say something like: Before we practice the whole passage, let's look at the second sentence. The second sentence tells three things about jellyfish. There is a comma between each of those things. Touch each comma.

  The comma tells us to pause a little. Follow along with your finger as I read the sentence. Watch for the commas and listen to me pause. "Jellyfish have no bones, clear bodies, and no brains."

  Guide practice with your voice.

  Try reading the sentence with me. Jellyfish have no bones, clear bodies, and no brains.

  Have students read the sentence, independent of your voice.

  Read the sentence without me. (Jellyfish have no bones, clear bodies, and no brains.)

- Demonstrate expressive, fluent reading of the passage.
- Guide practice with your voice.
- Have students read the passage, independent of your voice.
- Time individual students.

Note: If students have Strong Passes on assessments, you may wish to skip the Fluency Passage.

❺ DAILY STORY READING—See Daily Lesson Planning.

❻ COMPREHENSION AND SKILL ACTIVITIES—See Daily Lesson Planning.

Unit 47 Exercise 6

For use with Story 6 as needed

1. SOUND REVIEW Use the Sound Cards for Units 39–47 and selected Review Cards.

2. SOUND AND SENTENCE PRACTICE Have students read each sentence, then identify the words with underlined sounds. Next, read the underlined sounds.

ex	My dog took a big bite out of the balloon and it exploded! The explosion was so loud it hurt my ears. We don't want any more balloons to explode.

3. ACCURACY/FLUENCY BUILDING For each section, have students read any underlined part, then read each word. Next, have students read the whole column and identify what's the same about each word. ADVANCED ACCURACY/FLUENCY Have students read the word first, then read the underlined sound.

A1 Sound Practice	B1 Consonant Blends	C1 Multisyllabic Words	D1 Changing Words	E1 Tricky Words
point	scr-eech	station	knew	love
noise	scr-atch	appeared	know	wonder
voice	scr-ap	allowed	now	fruit
soil	scr-ape	asteroids	pow	field
boat	scr-ub	excitement	paw	against
croak	scr-eam	tentacles	saw	metal
groan	scr-een	responded	fin	**E2** Question Words
moan	**B2** Bossy E	**C2** Rhyming Words	fine	who
A2 Morphographs	beside	caught	find	where
bicycle	inflate	taught	kind	what
unlock	excite	head	kit	why
careful	rewrite	read	knit	when
remade			knot	
			know	

4. ★ NEW WORDS IN CONTEXT: BRAINS, JELLYFISH, AND STING; FLUENCY PASSAGE See the Teacher's Guide.

Jellyfish

Jellyfish are interesting animals that live in the sea. 9
Jellyfish have no bones, clear bodies, and no brains. 18
Jellyfish have hundreds of tentacles that sting and 26
catch food. Jellyfish are at home in their deep sea 36
habitat. However, if a jellyfish were put on the moon, 46
it would be an alien. 51

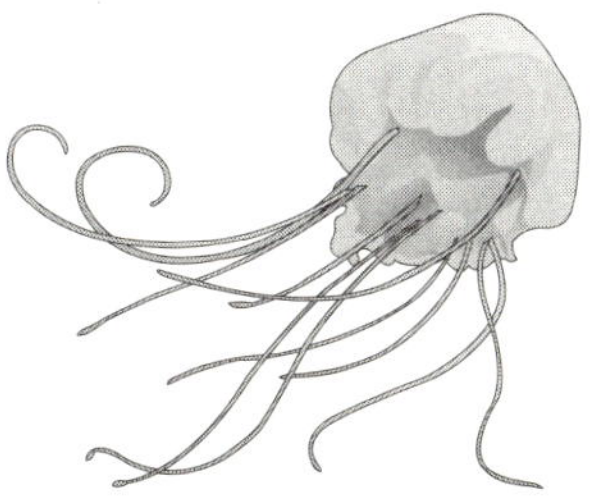

5. DAILY STORY READING

54

◆◆ SENTENCE SUGGESTIONS

(A1) noise—We heard a strange . . . *noise.*

(B1) scrape—When I fell off my bike, I got a . . . *scrape* on my knee.

(C2) caught—We spent all day chasing butterflies. Finally, we . . . *caught* one. Then we let it go.

(D1) fine—Her scratch looked like it hurt, but she said she was . . . *fine.*

(E1) field—We were going to play catch in the . . . *field.*

Sentence Suggestions: Use sentences *after* decoding the individual word. Using sentences emphasizes that words have meaning.

◆◆ Repeat and extend practice for English Language Learners and students with language delays.

PROCEDURES

1. Introduction

Have students summarize Chapters 1–5 by following the gray text in the storybook.

2. First Reading

- Mix group and individual turns, independent of your voice. Have students work toward an accuracy goal of 0–2 errors. Quietly keep track of errors made by all students in the group. Gently correct any error and have students reread the sentence.
- After reading the story, practice any difficult words.

3. Optional Repeated Readings

a. Short Passage Practice

Select short passages from the story. Demonstrate expressive, fluent reading. Guide practice with your voice. Then provide individual turns.

b. Timed Readings

As time allows, have students do Timed Readings while others follow along.

c. Partner Reading

During students' daily independent work, have them do Partner Reading.

4. Homework 6

Have students read the story at home. (*Read Well Plus* Homework is available in blackline masters.)

CHAPTER 6

A Problem in Space

What has happened so far?[1]

The rescue ball with the problem inside floated out into space. The whole class pressed up against the shuttle's windows. They could see the problem inside the ball. It ate the backpack. Then the problem stuck its mouth onto the rescue ball.

1 Summarizing—Main Characters, Problem, Action

(Asha brought a problem on the class field trip in her backpack. The problem ate everything in Asha's backpack—even her air tank. The teacher was afraid the air tank would blow up, so it sent the problem out into space in a rescue ball.)

"Stop!" yelled Maria. Then the problem took a big bite out of the rescue ball. It split open and the air whooshed out. The problem floated into space.

"Oh no!" everyone groaned, but the problem just kept on eating. Before anyone could say anything else, the air tank exploded, and the problem puffed up like a big balloon.

The class watched in silence, but the problem seemed fine. It ate the last shreds of the rescue ball. The problem spun around a couple of times as if to say, "Thanks for lunch!" Then it zoomed off into space.

Maria spoke first, "Oh wow! Problems can live in space."

Asha said, "Maybe the problems can be sent back into space. Maybe they'd like that."

"Does that mean we won't have problems anymore?" Maria asked.

"Well, I know I don't," said Asha.

Just then, as if nothing had happened, the teacher announced, "The shuttle will soon arrive at the asteroid mine." With so much excitement, the class had forgotten about the field trip.

The problem had zoomed off into space. What do you think the problem will do next?

❶ **Predicting**

FOCUS ON EXPRESSION

After completing the story, reread pages 20–21. Say something like: The ending of the story was very exciting. Let's reread pages 20–21. There is a lot of action in this part of the story. Page 20 starts out with Maria yelling when the problem takes a bite out of the rescue ball. Then the class groans when the problem keeps on eating. Finally, when the air tank explodes, the children grow quiet.

Listen to me read the first paragraph with expression. Then you take a turn.

Repeat with each paragraph. Demonstrate sentences. Have students read with you. Have students read individually.

COMPREHENSION BUILDING: ORAL STORY RETELL

◆◆ ELL students and students with language delays will benefit from the oral story retell. Students with strong English oral language skills can skip this activity and go directly to the written story map and written retell.

Have students study the pictures, then ask questions and discuss the pictures as indicated in the storybook in light gray text. The diamond, circle, square, and triangle provide visual references for the introduction, beginning, middle, and end of the story.

Summarizing
Sequencing →

STORY SUMMARY

A PROBLEM IN A BACKPACK

◆ Who was the story about?[1]
Where did the girls live?[2]

● What happened at the beginning of the story?[3]

■ What happened in the middle of the story?[4]

▲ What happened at the end of the story?[5]

22

1. **Identifying—Who (Main Characters)** (The story was about Asha and Maria.)
2. **Identifying—Where** (The girls lived on a space station.)
3. **Explaining—Beginning** (Asha and Maria's class went on a field trip to an asteroid mine. Asha told Maria she had a problem in her backpack.)
4. **Explaining—Middle** (Asha had a small alien that she called "a problem" in her backpack. The alien ate everything in her backpack, including an air tank. Asha didn't want her teacher, a robot, to know about the problem.)
5. **Explaining—End** (The teacher had Asha put her backpack in a rescue ball. Then the teacher released the problem into space. Everyone was happy to find out that the alien could live in space.)

STORY MAP

As appropriate, make an overhead (BLM copy) of Activity 10 to demonstrate or guide how to complete the story map.

Summarizing
Sequencing/ Complete Sentence, Conventions—Beginning Capital, Period

Identifying—Main Characters Describing

Explaining—Beginning, Action

Explaining—Middle, Problem, Action

Explaining—End, Conclusion

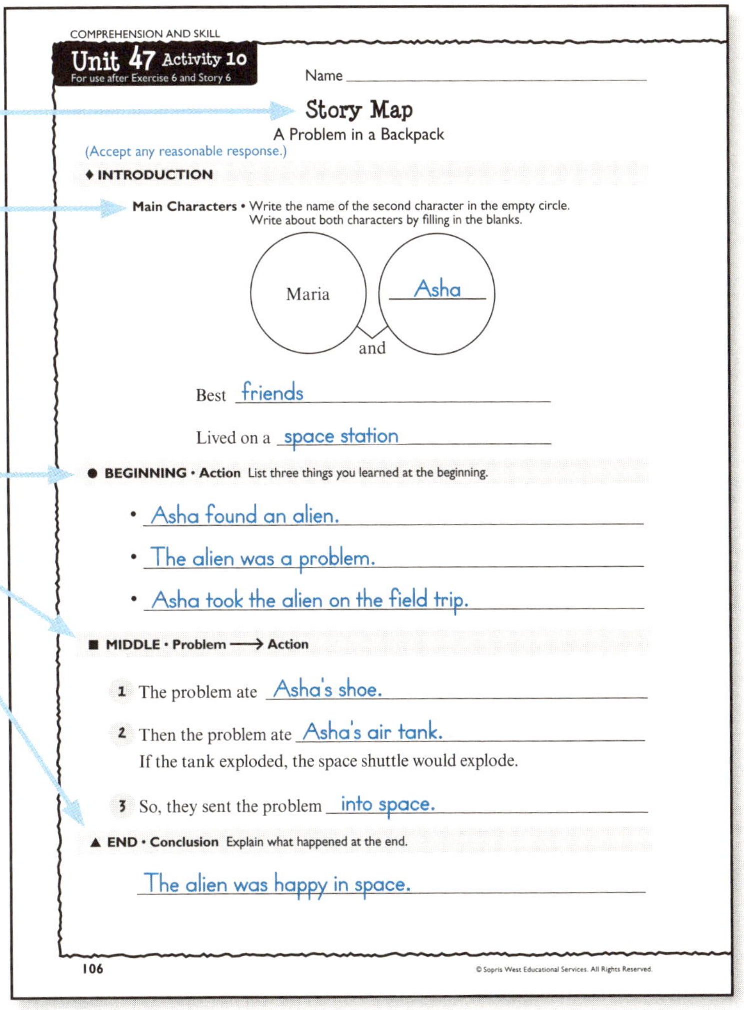

COMPREHENSION AND SKILL

Unit 47 Activity 10
For use after Exercise 6 and Story 6

Name ______

Story Map
A Problem in a Backpack

(Accept any reasonable response.)

♦ INTRODUCTION

Main Characters • Write the name of the second character in the empty circle. Write about both characters by filling in the blanks.

Maria and Asha

Best friends

Lived on a space station

● BEGINNING • Action List three things you learned at the beginning.

- Asha found an alien.
- The alien was a problem.
- Asha took the alien on the field trip.

■ MIDDLE • Problem ⟶ Action

1 The problem ate Asha's shoe.

2 Then the problem ate Asha's air tank.
If the tank exploded, the space shuttle would explode.

3 So, they sent the problem into space.

▲ END • Conclusion Explain what happened at the end.

The alien was happy in space.

106

CHECKOUT OPPORTUNITY

Listen to your students read individually while others work.

PROCEDURES

For each step, demonstrate and guide practice as needed.

Story Map—Basic Instructions

- Using the overhead (BLM copy) of the story map, demonstrate and guide how to complete each section of the activity—main characters, beginning, middle, and end. For some groups, provide students with time to complete each section of their own story map before you demonstrate and guide how to complete the next section.
- For more independent writers, demonstrate and guide how to write the entire story map, then have students complete their own story map independently.

Note: Remind students that a sentence begins with a capital letter and ends with a period.

WRITTEN RETELL

Use an overhead (BLM copy) of a completed Activity 10 story map and an enlarged (BLM copy) of Activity 11 to demonstrate how to complete the written retell.

Summarizing
Sequencing
Complete Sentence,
Conventions—Beginning Capital, Period

Identifying—Main Characters
Describing

Explaining—Beginning, Action

Explaining—Middle, Problem, Action

COMPREHENSION AND SKILL
Unit 47 Activity 11
For use after Exercise 6 and Story 6

Name ____________

Written Retell
A Problem in a Backpack

♦ **INTRODUCTION • Main Characters** Introduce Maria and Asha. Write about both characters.

Maria and Asha were best friends. They lived on a space station. They even went to a space school.

● **BEGINNING •** Explain how the story started.

One day, Asha found an alien. The alien was a problem. It ate everything. Asha took the alien on the school field trip.

■ **MIDDLE • Problem ⟶ Action** Describe what the problem did, what happened, and what they did about it.

On the space shuttle, the alien kept eating. It ate Asha's shoe and her air tank. Finally, the teacher sent the problem into space.

 107

MANAGEABLE SEGMENTS
(Reminder)

If needed, divide the written retell into manageable segments.

- For some groups, provide students with time to write each section of their own retell before you demonstrate and guide how to complete the next section—introduction, beginning, middle, and end.
- For more independent writers, demonstrate and guide how to write the entire retell and then have students complete their own retell independently.

PROCEDURES

Written Retell—Basic Instructions

Demonstrate and guide how to use the story map from Activity 10 to create a written retell.

- Using the overhead (BLM copy) of the story map, show how to construct an introductory paragraph.
  Guide how to write sentences to introduce the story, based on the information in students' story maps.
  Based on the story map, demonstrate and guide how to describe the characters.
- Repeat for the beginning, middle, and end of the story.
- Have students explain why they liked or didn't like the story in Story Response.
- Have students illustrate any part of "A Problem in a Backpack" in the box.

COMPREHENSION AND SKILL

Unit 47 Activity 11
(continued)

Name ____________________

Explaining—End, Conclusion → ■ **END** • Explain what happened at the end.

Everyone was worried, but the alien was happy in space.

Responding
Explaining → **STORY RESPONSE** • Start with *I liked the story because …* or *I didn't like the story because …*

I liked the story because the author has a good imagination.

Visualizing, Illustrating → **ILLUSTRATION** • Draw a picture of the story in the box.

108

End of the Unit

In this section, you will find:

Making Decisions

As you near the end of the unit, you will need to make decisions. Should you administer the Oral Reading Fluency Assessment or should you teach Extra Practice lessons?

Unit 47 Oral Reading Fluency Assessment

The Unit 47 Oral Reading Fluency Assessment is located on page 62.

End-of-the-Unit Celebration

PROCEDURES

Before copying the certificate and parent letter, determine how you wish to complete the letter. A few options follow:

- You may wish to conserve instructional time by filling out the parent letter before copying it.
  1. Write "Parents" in the salutation line and "Small problems can become big problems" for the lesson learned.
  2. Write a group accomplishment such as "We are especially proud that everyone followed along when someone else was reading."
  3. Copy the blackline master. Fill in individual student information at the top of the certificate. Then have students co-sign the letter before taking it home.
- You may wish to conserve instructional time by filling out the parent letter in advance, tailoring the accomplishment for each child.
  1. Complete the salutation line and lesson learned, then copy the blackline master.
  2. Tailor the accomplishment for each child. For example, an individual's accomplishment might be helping a friend sound out a difficult word.
  3. Fill in individual student information at the top of the certificate. Then have students co-sign the letter before taking it home.
- You may wish to use group time to have students fill out the parent letter.
  1. Quickly brainstorm with students the lesson learned and a group accomplishment.
  2. Have students fill in the salutation line, the lesson learned, and the group accomplishment. Then have them co-sign the letter.

Note: If a student lives with a single parent or a guardian, tailor the salutation line as appropriate.

Extra Practice

Lessons and blackline masters for added decoding practice and fluency work are provided for students who need extended practice opportunities.

Making Decisions

ASSESSMENT READINESS

- Assess when students are able to easily complete tasks from the beginning of a lesson.
- If students are not ready for the assessment, proceed to the Extra Practice lessons.

GENERAL ASSESSMENT GUIDELINES

- Assess all students individually.
- Score student responses on the Student Assessment Record, adhering to the scoring criteria in the assessment section of *Getting Started.* Use a stopwatch to gauge WCPM.

STRONG PASS OPTIONS

- If students read with 100% accuracy and exceed 109 words correct per minute, consider shortening the number of days spent per lesson. However, if students are benefiting from the written and oral comprehension activities, continue with the current pace of instruction.
- If an individual reads with significantly greater fluency than others in the group, consider regrouping.

PASS

Continue with the current pace of instruction. Consider increasing fluency practice.

WEAK PASS OPTIONS

- If more than one student is accurate but not fluent:
  a. Provide the Extra Practice lessons with added practice on any specific skills missed.
  b. In the next units, begin each story reading with a review of the previous day's story. After reading the story, include Short Passage Practice on a daily basis.
- If an individual child is accurate but not fluent:
  a. Set up five-minute tutorials on a daily basis with an assistant, trained volunteer, or cross-age tutor. Have the tutor provide Short Passage Practice and Timed Readings.
  b. Find ways to provide a double dose of *Read Well* instruction.
     Have the student work in his or her group *and* a lower group.
     Have an instructional assistant, older student, or parent volunteer preview or review lessons.
     Have an instructional assistant provide instruction with Extra Practice lessons.

NO PASS OPTIONS—FLUENT BUT NOT ACCURATE

- If a student makes three or more errors on an *isolated* skill or word, but fluency is within the passing range, reteach the skill and move forward.
- If a student makes three or more errors on *varied* skills, but fluency is within the passing range, reteach the unit or provide Extra Practice lessons with added practice on any difficult skills and an increased focus on accurate reading.

NO PASS OPTIONS—NOT FLUENT AND/OR THREE CONSECUTIVE WEAK PASSES

- If a student fails the fluency requirements for a Pass on three consecutive units, re-evaluate placement.
- If a student fails the fluency requirements for a Pass on three consecutive units, provide a quick Jell-Well Review of all vowel units, starting with *Read Well 1*, Unit 16. When the Jell-Well Review is complete, reteach and reassess previously taught *Read Well Plus* units.

END-OF-THE-UNIT CELEBRATION

When students pass the assessment, celebrate with the Certificate of Achievement. (See page 63.)

Note: Using the Flesch-Kincaid Grade Level readability formula, the Unit 47 Assessment has a 2.6 readability level.

TRICKY WORD WARM-UP

brought	field	worry	thought	alien

ORAL READING FLUENCY PASSAGE

It Is Back

★Matt really liked the class field trip. A friend had 10
brought an alien onto the shuttle. Everyone worried that 19
the alien would explode. Matt's teacher sent it into space, 29
and Matt thought he would never see it again. 38

When Matt got home, he started to tell his dad all 49
about the trip. His dad got a very funny look on his face. 62
Then Matt's dad said, "I can tell you what the alien looks 74
like. In fact, I can show you." 81

Matt followed his dad out to the field where they 91
played baseball. Matt was surprised to see a hungry 100
alien, but it wasn't just any alien. It was the alien from 112
the spacecraft. It gave a snort, hoot, and squeak. 121

Matt said with excitement, "I think it really likes me." 131

Matt's dad said, "Yes, but I'm worried. It's still a 141
problem. What do you think we should do?" 149

ORAL READING FLUENCY	Start timing at the ★. Mark errors. Make a single slash in the text (/) at 60 seconds. If the student completes the passage in less than 60 seconds, have the student go back to the ★ and continue reading. Make a double slash (//) in the text at 60 seconds.
WCPM	Determine words correct per minute by subtracting errors from words read in 60 seconds.
STRONG PASS	The student scores no more than 2 errors on the first pass through the passage and reads a minimum of 109 or more words correct per minute. Proceed to Unit 48.
PASS	The student scores no more than 2 errors on the first pass through the passage and reads 88 to 108 words correct per minute. Proceed to Unit 48.
WEAK PASS	The student scores no more than 2 errors on the first pass through the passage and reads 68 to 87 words correct per minute. Proceed to Unit 48 with added fluency practice, and/or provide a Jell-Well Review.
NO PASS	The student scores 3 or more errors on the first pass through the passage and/or reads 67 or fewer words correct per minute. Provide added fluency practice and/or a Jell-Well Review, then retest.

Congratulations!

____
Name

On this ______________ day of ______________, ________,

you have successfully completed *Read Well Plus*, Unit 47.

Skills • Sounds: s, e, ee, m, a, d, th, n, t, w, i, Th, h, c, r, ea, sh, k, -ck, oo, ar, wh, e (short), -y (as in "fly"), l, o, b, all, g, f, u, er, oo (as in "book"), y, a (schwa), p, ay, v, q, j, x, or, z, a_e, -y (as in "baby"), i_e, ou, ow (as in "cow"), ch, ai, igh, o_e, ir, aw, ew, u_e, ow (as in "snow"), ge, ci, ce, kn, ph, oa, oi, ea (as in "bread")

Skills • Affixes: -ed, -en, -er, -es, -est, -ing, -ly, -s, -y, -tion, re-, un-, ex-, -ful, bi-, de-, -able

Unit 47 Assessment: ______ words correct per minute

Dear ______________________________,

In this unit, we read a story about a girl who finds a funny alien that eats too much. The story tells about how Asha tries to deal with her little "problem."

The lesson we learned from this story is:

____

____

We are especially proud: ______________________________

____

____

Sincerely, ______________________________

and ______________________________

My Reading Record

- A Problem in a Backpack
- Frog and Toad Together
- A Class of Their Own
- Nate the Great
- Maya the Magnificent
- Carlos the Curious
- Why the Sloth Is Slow
- How the Camel Got His Hump
- How the Chipmunk Got His Stripes

❶ EXERCISE 6 REVIEW

For items 1–4, mix group and individual turns, independent of your voice.

❷ SENTENCE COMPLETION

Harry *paints.*

- Write the word "Harry" on the board and have students copy it.
- Have students read the beginning of the sentence with you. Say something like:
  The first part of the sentence tells who or what the sentence is about.
  Who or what is the sentence about? (Harry)
  The last part of the sentence tells what Harry does in the sentence.
  Harry paints everything red.
- Dictate the word "paints."
  The word is "paints." We're going to count the sounds in "paints."
  Tell me the first sound. **Hold up one finger.** (/p/)
  Repeat with /ai/, /nnn/, /t/, and /sss/.
  How many sounds are in "paints"? (Five)

  Tell me the first sound. (/p/) Write it.
  Tell me the next sound. (/ai/) Write it with the letters a and i.
  Tell me the next sound. (/nnn/) Write it.
  Tell me the next sound. (/t/) Write it.
  Tell me the next sound. (/sss/) Write it.
  Do Smooth Blending. (/painnntsss/) Read the word. (paints)
- Have students complete the sentence with a period.
- Have students read the sentence.

❸ DAILY STORY READING

1. First and Repeated Readings

Have students read the passage, mixing group and individual turns. Demonstrate expressive, fluent reading. Guide practice with your voice, then provide individual turns. As time allows, have students do Timed Readings while others follow along.

2. Partner Reading—Checkout Opportunity

CAUTION

Your students may not need Extra Practice. If in doubt, assess students and include Extra Practice only if needed.

DICTATION

- Demonstrate and guide practice as needed.
- Have students check and correct.

Name_______________________________

FLUENCY PASSAGE

Space School

Asha and Maria go to a space school. It is a very 12
exciting place. They study asteroids, new stars, and even 21
aliens. 22

The only thing that Asha and Maria don't like about 32
space school is their teacher's voice. It never really changes. 42
It goes on and on, just like a robot. Well, that isn't really a 56
surprise. The teacher talks like a robot because it is a robot! 68

Asha and Maria decided they would just have to put up 79
with the teacher's voice. After all, it is a pretty good teacher. 91

My personal best is _____ words correct per minute.
My goal is to read with 0–2 errors. This is what I did:

Have students read the sentences. Time individual students for 60 seconds; mark errors. To determine words correct per minute (WCPM), count words read in 60 seconds, subtract errors, and record on the chart. If the student completes the passage in less than 60 seconds, have him or her return to the top and continue reading. (Repeated readings may be completed with older students, assistants, or parents.)

Reading	1st	2nd	3rd	4th
Errors				
Words/ 60 seconds				
WCPM				

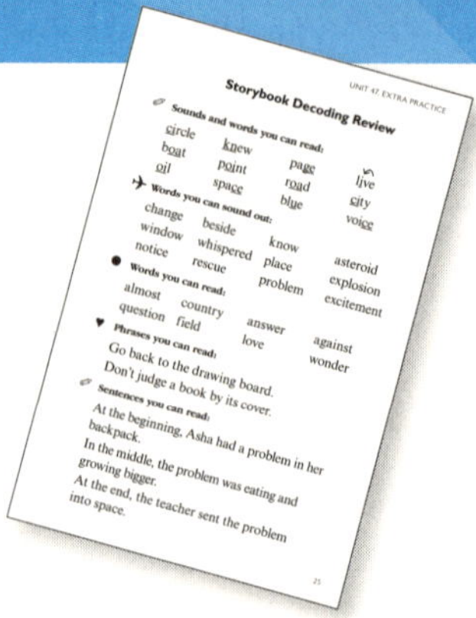
UNIT 47 EXTRA PRACTICE

Storybook Decoding Review

Sounds and words you can read:

circle	knew	page	live
boat	point	road	city
oil	space	blue	voice

Words you can sound out:

change	beside	know	asteroid
window	whispered	place	explosion
notice	rescue	problem	excitement

Words you can read:

almost	country	answer	against
question	field	love	wonder

Phrases you can read:

Go back to the drawing board.

Don't judge a book by its cover.

Sentences you can read:

At the beginning, Asha had a problem in her backpack.

In the middle, the problem was eating and growing bigger.

At the end, the teacher sent the problem into space.

❶ STORYBOOK DECODING REVIEW

For each row, mix group and individual turns, independent of your voice.

❷ SENTENCE COMPLETION

Annie *cooks*.

- Write the word "Annie" on the board and have students copy it.
- Have students read the beginning of the sentence with you.
- Ask students who the sentence is about. Tell students Annie cooks great pancakes.
- Dictate the word "cooks."
- Have students complete the sentence with a period and read the sentence.

CAUTION

Your students may not need Extra Practice. If in doubt, assess students and include Extra Practice only if needed.

❸ DAILY STORY READING

1. First and Repeated Readings

For each passage, have students read the passage, mixing group and individual turns. Demonstrate expressive, fluent reading. Guide practice with your voice, then provide individual turns. As time allows, have students do Timed Readings while others follow along.

2. Partner Reading—Checkout Opportunity

EXTRA PRACTICE 3

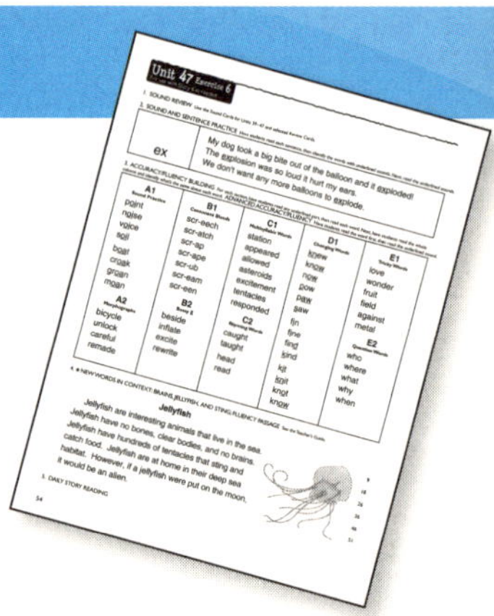

❶ EXERCISE 6 REVIEW

For items 1–4, mix group and individual turns, independent of your voice.

❷ SENTENCE COMPLETION

Fang *digs*.

- Write the word "Fang" on the board and have students copy it.
- Have students read the beginning of the sentence with you.
- Ask students who the sentence is about. Tell students Fang digs holes.
- Dictate the word "digs."
- Have students complete the sentence with a period and read the sentence.

❸ DAILY STORY READING

1. First and Repeated Readings

Have students read the passage, mixing group and individual turns. Demonstrate expressive, fluent reading. Guide practice with your voice, then provide individual turns. As time allows, have students do Timed Readings while others follow along.

2. Partner Reading—Checkout Opportunity

Name____________________

FLUENCY PASSAGE A

Robot Teacher

The robot decided to teach the class all about the aliens 11
that were going to come and visit the space school. It 22
announced, "We are going to study the alien problems. What 32
do you already know about the problems?" Asha was having 42
trouble keeping her mind on what the teacher was saying. 52

FLUENCY PASSAGE B

The Alien Problems

The robot teacher decided to teach the children all 9
about the problems. It talked and talked and talked. The 19
robot said that the hungry little problems lived millions of 29
miles away on a tiny blue planet. The aliens had to leave 41
their planet because of an explosion. They were in search 51
of a new home. 55

My personal best is _____ words correct per minute.
My goal is to read with 0–2 errors. This is what I did:

Reading	1st	2nd	3rd	4th
Errors				
Words/ 30 seconds				
WCPM				

Have students read the sentences. Time individual students for 30 seconds on one passage; mark errors. To determine words correct per minute (WCPM), count words read in 30 seconds, subtract errors, multiply times two, and record on the chart. If the student completes the passage in less than 30 seconds, have him or her return to the top and continue reading. (Repeated readings may be completed with older students, assistants, or parents.)

Name________________________________

FLUENCY PASSAGE

A New Voice

The robot teacher was busy teaching the children about 9
the fascinating little aliens. It asked, "Does anyone have a 19
question?" There was silence in the classroom. It asked, 28
"Why did the problems come visit us?" No one responded. 38
Everyone was asleep! Finally, the robot teacher sadly said, 47
"It is time for a new teacher." 54

Asha and Maria were unhappy. Asha said to her mom, 64
"We have a problem. Our teacher's voice is so old and worn 76
out, it puts us to sleep. The teacher thinks we need a new 89
robot. What shall we do?" 94

Asha's mom said, "I just read about a new voice box 105
for old robots like your teacher. Let's get everyone together 115
and buy your teacher a new voice!" 122

My personal best is _____ words correct per minute.
My goal is to read with 0–2 errors. This is what I did:

Have students read the sentences. Time individual students for 60 seconds; mark errors. To determine words correct per minute (WCPM), count words read in 60 seconds, subtract errors, and record on the chart. If the student completes the passage in less than 60 seconds, have him or her return to the top and continue reading. (Repeated readings may be completed with older students, assistants, or parents.)

Reading	1st	2nd	3rd	4th
Errors				
Words/ 60 seconds				
WCPM				